Playwrights for Tomorrow

VOLUME 8

A Gun Play

BY YALE M. UDOFF

Anniversary on Weedy Hill

BY ALLEN JOSEPH

The Nihilist

BY WILLIAM N. MONSON

EDITED, WITH AN INTRODUCTION, BY ARTHUR H. BALLET

PLAYWRIGHTS FOR TOMORROW

A Collection of Plays, Volume 8

THE UNIVERSITY OF MINNESOTA PRESS • MINNEAPOLIS

Printed in the United States of America at
North Central Publishing Co., St. Paul

Library of Congress Catalog Card Number: 66-19124

ISBN 0-8166-0652-8

PUBLISHED IN THE UNITED KINGDOM AND INDIA BY OXFORD UNIVERSITY PRESS, LONDON AND DELHI, AND IN CANADA BY THE COPP CLARK PUBLISHING CO. LIMITED, TORONTO

These volumes of *Playwrights for Tomorrow* are respectfully and lovingly dedicated to the late Sir Tyrone Guthrie — a friend, an inspiration, and a very great man of the theatre

Playwrights for Tomorrow

VOLUME 8

INTRODUCTION

Arthur H. Ballet

As Sabina in Thornton Wilder's *Skin of Our Teeth* says: "Oh — why can't we have plays like we used to have — *Peg o' My Heart*, and *Smilin' Thru*, and *The Bat* . ." Well, Sabina, we still do have plays like that. Playwrights write them and theatres do them. Despite protests to the contrary, I rather suspect that writers, audiences, and theatres really do want "plays like we used to have . . good entertainment with a message you can take home with you!"

The Office for Advanced Drama Research (O.A.D.R.) has tried to find new voices and daring theatres to produce the different plays. The O.A.D.R. was established in 1963 at the University of Minnesota, with financial aid from the Rockefeller Foundation, to provide an opportunity for playwrights seeking to try fresh paths, an opportunity to have their work performed without the pressures endemic to the commercial theatre. At first productions were limited to the Minneapolis–St. Paul area, but the program was expanded in 1969 and since then productions have been staged under O.A.D.R. aegis in many parts of the country.

It takes a steady hand to run the O.A.D.R. program. After reading literally thousands of unproduced plays during the several years of directing the O.A.D.R., I'm not so sure my hand is nearly as sure as it used to be. I'm shaken to find myself now reading imitation Megan Terry, Terrence McNally, Sam Shepard, Jean-Claude van Itallie, Maria Irene Fornés, and Rochelle Owens. It seems only last week I was trying to get theatres to take a fling with those writers, and now would-be playwrights are imitating them.

Stranger still to have some of the very theatres which rejected those

3

"famous" playwrights seven years ago when I sent their work to them now returning to me new work by others with testy little notes reminding me of their interest only in quality work such as that of Megan Terry. The world does whirl.

Strangest perhaps of all to read the directors' rejections of the new scripts sent to them. Their criticism tends to lament the lack of "style" in our native writers. (The assumption here is that only the British can really write anyway.) Or they condemn the "inept theatre sense" of the playwrights of today. Or they inform me that they are really looking for "experimentation." I shudder in disbelief when I see the stage work of those very critical directors. If the new writers are somewhat lacking (and indeed they may be), so are the directors themselves. They too sometimes fall short of "style" and "theatre sense" and even a smidgen of theatrical daring. But *they* have the theatres, and playwrights need their theatres — whereas directors, incompetent or otherwise, don't really need living playwrights.

Is it any wonder that I often question my skill at the delicate task of finding playwrights and theatres which can somehow come together effectively, with the generous financial assistance of the Rockefeller Foundation as administered by the University of Minnesota. Fortunately, though, there are just enough theatres willing and able to take a chance and enough writers creatively exploring the world around them to make the work exciting and even stabilizing — some of the time.

The plays and playwrights in these two simultaneously issued volumes, numbers 8 and 9, of *Playwrights for Tomorrow* are a mixed bag in every way: young and old, experienced and inexperienced, collegiate and professional, and small as well as large in endeavor, in scope, in passion, and in vision. But of the thousands I've read and the scores we've managed to get staged, these works more or less represent where the action seems to be at the moment.

Yale Udoff's *A Gun Play* went the whole route for the O.A.D.R. After I had read it and sent it to a number of theatres, Paul Weidner of the Hartford Stage Company had the great good sense to be struck by the potential of the play. He staged it most successfully in Connecticut, where commercial producers optioned the play after the *New York Times* critic Mel Gussow had commended it. These producers eventually brought it to New York City for an off-Broadway run which raised hackles in some quarters and high praise in others. Clive Barnes, also of the *Times*, proclaimed its importance and loyally supported the play through a precarious run. Udoff, a professional writer primarily involved in the mass media, probably has turned an important corner in his career and for the theatre.

Chiefly a professional actor in film and television, Allen Joseph turned to playwriting in the midst of a well-established career in the theatre. The result, *Anniversary on Weedy Hill*, is clearly a work for the theatre. Produced by Theatre West, a company of earnest and dedicated professionals in West Hollywood, the play had an excellent cast and was itself funny, true, honest, and very affecting on stage — as it is in reading. One unusual note: about a year after this production, one of the actors in *Anniversary on Weedy Hill*, Hal Lynch, wrote a play himself and it was presented, again with support from the O.A.D.R., at — of all places — Theatre West.

The Nihilist by William N. Monson was the second play the O.A.D.R. offered through the facilities of the University of California at Davis Theatre under the direction of Alfred Rossi. And once again this academic theatre brought a vitality and an immediacy to a play drawing richly on history. Monson, himself from the world of academe, benefited from Rossi's theatrical staging of the play — which burst the physical confines of the theatre. The play here published reflects that learning and that sense of what a play can achieve in a theatre.

David Korr's *Encore* and Gladden Schrock's *Madam Popov* were originally scheduled as a double bill at the Other Place Theatre of The Tyrone Guthrie Theater in Minneapolis, but the director and company so enjoyed working with the individual writers that eventually the evenings were expanded, and each playwright's work was performed as a separate entity. The 1970 season at the Guthrie was sadly lackluster — except for the work of the Other Place Theatre's young company and these two writers. A number of pleasantly unprejudiced individuals indicated that Korr and Schrock provided the best theatre in town that summer — and certainly I'll agree.

Children of the Kingdom by Don Keith Opper is the result of close coopera-tion between playwright, company, and director. The Company Theatre in Los Angeles and its gifted, imaginative director, Steven Kent, nurtured the concept with Opper and together they made exciting, incisive theatre. The O.A.D.R.'s function was simply to encourage a very young and creative writer and to aid his theatre in realizing that potential.

In considering Joel Schwartz's work I admit bias: a few years ago he was a graduate student working under my direction at the University of

Minnesota. An earlier play, written at Minnesota and produced successfully there and at the Mark Taper Forum in Los Angeles, bore the promise of an important talent. *Psalm of Two Davids*, though, struck me as a major breakthrough for this writer and for playwriting generally. It pointed a new direction: almost neoclassic in form and yet reflecting a kind of mysticism and spaced-out insight, this work was rejected by dozens of theatres — for one reason or another. Finally, Jim Dunn at the College of Marin in California read it and flipped. His production at the two-year college was, without much doubt, one of the most impressive productions of any play in the O.A.D.R.'s repertory. A mixed audience packed the theatre night after night and accorded the play a standing ovation. In addition to providing a first-rank writer with a first-rank production, this experience disproved old fears about new plays at tiny schools. But then of course not many small schools have Jim Dunns directing their productions — indeed, lamentably very few large schools have Jim Dunns, either.

As these volumes go off to the printer, the future of the O.A.D.R. is unpredictable. The plays continue to arrive, and I read them all. The theatres continue to say they want to do new plays, and I try to help find them, but I sometimes think they really want *King Lear* or *Smilin' Through*. And the writers are quite often represented by literary agents who set up impossible — not to say stupid — barriers to production. The Rockefeller Foundation is thinking about trying other ways to help playwrights, and so is the O.A.D.R. Meanwhile, my own hand now and then feels a shade less steady than it used to feel. Even as the trembling begins, though, I know it's been worth it. I hope the reader — and the producer — agree. Theatre is little more than a shaky stab in the dark that sometimes strikes magnificent sparks. We try.

YALE M. UDOFF

A Gun Play

to the memory of Igor Stravinsky

The Setting

The action takes place in a small club in a large American city. The club — part discotheque, part coffee house — encompasses the entire stage, is semicircular in form, and thrusts out and into the audience. Arcing right from down center are three large round four-chaired tables; to the left of down center is a small two-chaired table, some empty space, then two more two-chaired tables which sit next to the wall but do not extend past center left. In the corner down left is a tall, many-tiered pastry stand. Where center left starts to arc toward upper left is the maître d's stand: it is angled toward the audience and has a small lamp above it. Behind the stand, built into the wall, is a console of assorted dials that control the piped-in music, movie screen and projection apparatus, etc. A little past the maître d's stand is the vestibule entrance to the club (and the offstage coatroom). At the top of the arc — upper center — is a large round disc that serves as both mirror and, when opened, movie screen. A little past this disc is a swinging door marked "Kitchen." As the arc curves toward upper right, it comes upon two transparent doors, one labeled "Men," the other "Women." Both wash/powder rooms can be seen into; however, inside each room is another door leading to the offstage toilets. Near these rooms hangs a pay phone. All wall areas not occupied by doors, signs, etc., are covered with mirrors. Stage center is empty and serves as the dance floor. It is evening.

A GUN PLAY

The stage is set but empty. Overhead lights are dim. The stage remains like this for at least a minute. Presently, we hear the rattle of pots and pans as out of the kitchen shuffles Stan, wearing a white apron, waiter-style, and carrying an old water bucket (which is with him throughout the evening, used mainly to bail water in the kitchen — the sound of which is easily heard — as well as for assorted jobs such as carrying ashtrays to tables). He wearily glances around the club, checks his watch, shakes his head, surprised the place is still empty. He moves around, checking to see if there's anything he hasn't attended to. Finally he reaches the maître d's stand; from the way he relates to it, dusting, switching on the light, opening the reservation book — in fact almost caressing the stand — we understand that for him this is where all power and authority resides. From inside the stand he pulls a group of small vases, each holding one rose, and a number of ashtrays. He moves through the club, placing one vase and one ashtray on each table. Finished, he checks his watch, moves toward the pastry table. Pause. A pastry tray is missing. Upset, Stan moves quickly into the kitchen. From the vestibule an elegant and imperious Orlando strides into the heart of the club. (He's come from the offstage coatroom and is dressed for the evening: the usual maître d's uniform, tuxedo and all.) The manner in which he surveys the club immediately tells us he's the crown prince of this country. His eyes check everything quickly. He spots the pastry table, moves to it, and glares at the naked spot that should have held the missing pastries. Stan reenters, carrying a large pastry tray. He spots Orlando, knows he's in trouble. Orlando turns to him. Stan moves slowly toward the pastry table, halts.

ORLANDO

You're late with that tray by twenty minutes!

STAN

(*indicating the empty tables*) So what difference?

ORLANDO

All the difference. (*Orlando has so positioned himself as to prevent Stan from putting down the tray. Three times he attempts to put it down and three times he is rebuffed.*)

STAN

May I put it down, please!

ORLANDO

Why! (*Pause. Orlando steps aside.*) Well, what are you waiting for! Put it down. Put it down . . Stan*ley*!

STAN

You know I don't like to be called Stanley. Don't call me that way. Call me Stan . . if you don't mind. (*slight pause*)

ORLANDO

All you had to do was ask. (*Stan slams the tray onto the table. Orlando moves to his stand, busies himself with the reservation book.*) No reservations tonight?

STAN

No.

ORLANDO

Why not!

STAN

Maybe people want to stay at home. Be by themselves.

ORLANDO

Ridiculous! Check the wine cellar. Make sure we have more red wine than white. Let me know how many bottles of Château Maison are left. (*Stan disappears into the kitchen. Orlando again checks his stand, the reservation book, his watch, shakes his head in disgust. He uses dials to brighten the overhead light and add piped-in music. Offstage the sound of a door opening and closing, footsteps. Orlando hears, but busies himself. Wallace appears in the vestibule. He wears a dry trench coat and carries a large attaché case. He stands motionlessly, staring directly into the club, at the audience, but* not *at Orlando. Presently Orlando, having played the maître d's game, officially recognizes his new customer and moves to him.*) Ah! Good evening. You wish a table? (*Wallace doesn't answer, stares straight ahead.*) Your coat? (*Orlando moves to take his coat. Wallace, whose facial expression takes no account of Orlando, nevertheless puts down his attaché case and permits Orlando to help him with his coat. Orlando reaches for the attaché*

10

case; Wallace keeps it from him. Orlando shrugs a smile, moves to the offstage coatroom, returns, motions his customer to follow him, which he does carrying his attaché case, an unusually large one. Wallace is seated at the four-chaired table farthest away from down center, and sits facing the audience. He lays his case on another chair, in such a position to prevent the audience from seeing its contents when opened. Orlando presents the menu, smiles, returns to his stand. Wallace lets the menu lie on the table, ignoring it. He sits rigidly, staring straight ahead. Orlando turns the music up a few decibels. Stan comes through the kitchen door, carrying his bucket and wearing rubbers. He heads for Wallace, halts at his table, poised with pencil and pad. Wallace stares at Stan's rubbers.)

WALLACE

The rubbers — are they good?

STAN

Excuse me?

WALLACE

You're wearing rubbers (*Stan nods.*) I was given a pair . . last Christmas. Just like . . like them. Do they make your feet sweat?

STAN

I . . eh. To tell the truth —

WALLACE

(*interrupts*) Are they easy to pull off? (*suspicious*) They're not too tight. Do they keep the slush out? They don't leak, I hope.

STAN

Well, actually —

WALLACE

(*interrupts*) They don't stretch, do they? (*Stan nods no.*) You're sure? I want some soup.

STAN

What kind?

WALLACE

Soup. (*slight pause*)

STAN

Soup du jour? Potage mongol? . . (*Waits. No answer. Starts away.*)

WALLACE

No, coffee. Make it coffee. Hot coffee. (*Stan returns.*)

STAN

(*writing*) Make the soup coffee. (*magically whamming checkbook*) *Poof!* (*slight pause*) Cream and sugar? (*Wallace doesn't answer. Pause. Stan shrugs and moves toward the kitchen. Orlando halts him.*)

11

ORLANDO
What, may I ask, is the meaning of those filthy rubbers?

STAN
The wine cellar. It's flooding.

ORLANDO
(*calmly*) So.

STAN
My feet were getting wet.

ORLANDO
(*indicating Wallace*) Is anything wrong with that gentleman? What did he order?

STAN
Coffee.

ORLANDO
Only coffee! (*proudly*) Doesn't he know what type of an establishment this is? What kind of a place I run. Coffee?

STAN
He's okay. Been in once or twice. Never any trouble. He usually orders more later.

ORLANDO
So let it be. Coffee. To each his own. (*Stan disappears into the kitchen. Orlando returns to his stand. Offstage a door opens and closes, then footsteps. Lita appears first, Linden a step behind. Both wear raincoats that are soaked. They hold in the vestibule. Wallace ignores the newcomers. Orlando is at his stand, checking his book, playing the maître d's game.*)

LINDEN
If you like . . we could come back . . when it's more crowded.

LITA
Don't be silly. Who could I impress here anyway? It's simply a nice little place to let one's hair down. Everyone needs a place like that. (*Orlando chooses to recognize his customers and moves to them with his reservation book.*)

ORLANDO
Buena notte!

LITA
(*flustered*) But I thought you were French! (*to Linden*) I thought he was French . .

ORLANDO
(*kissing her hand*) Bon soir, mademoiselle!

LITA
(*to Linden*) See, I told you he was French.

12

A GUN PLAY

ORLANDO

A pleasure to have you again. (*Both start to remove their raincoats.*)

LITA

Why's the place so empty tonight? Very dreary. (*Orlando takes their dripping raincoats.*)

ORLANDO

The rain drives many away. C'est la vie. (*Orlando moves offstage with the coats. The two wait, both fidgeting with their clothes, their hair, etc. Suddenly, Lita reaches over to straighten out Linden's hair.*)

LINDEN

(*pulling away*) I'll do that! (*Orlando returns, opens his book.*)

ORLANDO

You have a reservation?

LINDEN

No.

ORLANDO

A sadness.

LITA

We forgot. Be nice to us, though.

ORLANDO

I'll see what can be managed. Mind you, I can in no way promise anything. (*moves to his stand, pores over his book, checking it with great solemnity*) I think we can work things out. Follow me, please. (*Leads them into the club and toward one table, but they move directly toward another, a four-chaired one at down center, and sit; Orlando returns to them, supplies the menu, waits.*)

LINDEN

Some Brie . . and a small bottle of red wine.

ORLANDO

Might I suggest, perhaps, a bottle of our superior house wine — Château Maison?

LINDEN

Yes.

LITA

No!

ORLANDO

(*to Linden, sympathetically*) C'est la vie. (*Orlando returns to his console. Wallace, separated from Lita and Linden by an empty table, determinedly arranges his table utensils. He uses his napkin to clean and polish his fork, before precisely setting it into place. He smiles, pleased. Stan moves out*

13

of the kitchen — wearing galoshes — and carrying a tray containing a pot of coffee, cup, and saucer.)

LINDEN

I don't understand why you like this place. It's nothing special. (*She slaps him hard across the face, fiddles with her mirror. Stan notices.*) Let's dance.

LITA

Linden, there's *no one* here.

LINDEN

Oh . . (*Stan arrives at Wallace's table. As he serves, Wallace immediately resets each piece.*)

WALLACE

I had to wait an hour that time. And still I didn't get it. And it hadn't been crowded — not at all. But they wouldn't give it to me. (*slight pause*) I stood. I kept standing. I wouldn't leave. (*slight pause*) Eventually, people left. Some did, at least. (*slight pause*) Then I sat . . but no one came. They ignored me. But I didn't leave. They didn't want me to come back. But I did. I came back. It was the same every night. (*slight pause*) Then one night . . it changed.

STAN

(*sympathetically*) Listen, in this world, what can you expect. Things change. (*Wallace pays no attention to Stan, who shrugs, starts for Lita and Linden, but is distracted by Orlando. He heads for the maître d'.*)

ORLANDO

(*indicating Wallace*) Nothing is wrong I hope. *You* assured me.

STAN

Like everyone he's got troubles. Nothing more and probably less.

ORLANDO

Still . .

STAN

Today, who doesn't have something wrong? In times like ours there's every reason.

ORLANDO

(*studying Wallace*) Well . . he dresses well. Got a nice smile. (*a building enthusiasm*) A fine-looking young man. Wholesome, well mannered, forceful when needed. Won't bore you with his opinions. (*slight pause*) A customer like that is good for business. You can go now. (*Stan starts away.*) Wait! (*Stan returns.*) Some Brie and a small bottle of red wine for the couple. Hurry! They've been waiting while you wasted my time.

STAN

What's the matter — don't they want a bottle of Château Maison?

14

A GUN PLAY

ORLANDO

Hurry! (*Stan trudges into the kitchen. Lita fiddles with her compact.*)

LITA

Have you seen Gloria Gill recently?

LINDEN

No.

LITA

I have. I saw her at Amy's the other night.

LINDEN

(*confused*) Amy's?

LITA

You *know* that Pam's left Roger?

LINDEN

Amy . . told you that.

LITA

Don't be ridiculous! How would Amy know Pam? Roz told me the story. (*chummy*) These days Pam and Roz are inseparable. Well, anyway, only two days after they'd separated I saw her with the most beautiful man. You know, the one who shares a tennis court with Jack. What's his name?

LINDEN

(*brightly*) Jack Small!

LITA

No, not Jack! The other man. The beautiful man. (*deliberately*) What's his name?

LINDEN

(*cautious*) Oh, you mean . . the other fellow.

LITA

Yes. Right. You get two gold stars. The other man — what's his name?

LINDEN

I don't think I know his name.

LITA

You *do* know Gloria?

LINDEN

Gloria who?

LITA

Gloria Gill!

LINDEN

No. (*She runs her finger over his perfect nose.*)

LITA

Ever thought of becoming a male model? It's got to be a lot more fun

15

than the stock market. (*He shrugs.*) We could have the same agents. Go to Peru on assignment together. I'd recommend you. I would. Really.

LINDEN

What's the head waiter's name? (*He pulls out a small black address book.*)

LITA

How should I know.

LINDEN

Stop acting like a goddamn whore!

LITA

All right. Don't get upset. Be nice.

LINDEN

If I knew his name. If I knew that — I mean, if you know the name of a bartender, a waiter, a maître d' . . well, you know, it helps. (*flips through the book*)

LITA

Helps what?

LINDEN

The names! (*slight pause*)

LITA

Orlando is the maître d', and the waiter is — is Stan . . ley.

LINDEN

(*writing*) You know, I really like this place.

LITA

You don't.

LINDEN

I do.

LITA

You're sure?

LINDEN

Positive. (*Stan slams out of the kitchen, moves toward Lita and Linden. Wallace lifts his case off the chair, places it on the table. He pulls it close to him, stares at it before finally opening it. He examines its contents, then pours himself coffee. Stan zips the bottle in front of Linden, pulling it back so quickly that identification of the label is impossible. The waiter then — with immense difficulty — uncorks the bottle, pours with a flourish. Tasting*) Thanks, Stanley.

STAN

If you don't mind, I prefer to be called Stan.

LINDEN

Sure. (*glances at Lita*) Anything you say. Thanks, Stan.

STAN

A pleasure. Will there be anything else?

LINDEN

No. But remember please, my name is Linden. For future reference, that is. (*pushes some crumpled bills into Stan's hand*)

STAN

For sure, Linden. Yes . . (*to himself*) *Linden?*

LINDEN

And Stan, the maître d', would you ask him to stop over, please.

STAN

A pleasure . . Linden. (*Stan moves to Orlando, whispers into his ear, then exits into the kitchen. Orlando heads for Linden.*)

ORLANDO

You requested me, monsieur.

LITA

See, he's French.

LINDEN

(*confidentially*) My name's Linden. Remember that please. For future use. (*He pushes money into Orlando's hand, who makes an elaborate cover movement so as to ensure that no one — himself included — spots the transaction.*)

ORLANDO

Of course, Mr. Linden, sir. You can count on me, on my discretion. Be assured your name is etched into my memory (*slight pause*) And *my* name, easy to remember, is Orlando. Linden! Ah yes . . Molto bene.

LINDEN

(*to Lita*) I thought you said he was French? (*She shrugs. Orlando returns to his stand. Wallace stops sipping his coffee and again focuses his attention on the contents of his open case. He closes the case, leaves it on the table, continues with his coffee. Lita rises, moves toward Wallace, suddenly changes direction, and heads for the powder room. She remains there, meticulously attending to her face, hair, etc. Offstage the front door opens, closes; footsteps. Jack and Norma move into the vestibule. Both wear drenched raincoats. Orlando knows they're waiting but is playing his maître d's game.*)

JACK

You said it, so don't deny it.

NORMA

I may have *implied* it, darling . . but never did I say it.

JACK

Liar.

NORMA

Projecting again. Sad.

JACK

C'mon — admit she upset you.

NORMA

Upset . .? (*Orlando arrives.*)

ORLANDO

And how are my two favorite regulars tonight?

NORMA

(*argumentively*) Just fine. Why ask!

ORLANDO

Oh . . no reason at all. (*to Jack*) We haven't seen much of you lately.

JACK

Very busy.

ORLANDO

Well now, that's always good to hear.

NORMA

Believe *everything* you hear.

ORLANDO

All . . according . . to who —

NORMA

Smile. Smile and the world is yours.

ORLANDO

Pardonnez?

NORMA

Forget it. (*Orlando takes both coats, moves offstage with them, returns, motions the couple to follow him toward the remaining four-chaired table. As they move, Norma speaks.*) Oh my, the place is jammed. (*They sit. Orlando hands them menus, returns to his stand. Lita leaves the powder room, halts immediately outside it. She scans the room, her eyes finally resting on Wallace.*)

JACK

All right — not upset, "bothered." Hmm?

NORMA

You know, Jack, I see you more than people I like.

JACK

Then why call so often?

NORMA

(*sweetly*) I know your number. (*slight pause*)

JACK

You know, you're a big girl now, Norma. You don't have to do what you don't want anymore. You've been around for *a long* time . .

18

A GUN PLAY

NORMA

I see you, dear, for many reasons. Most of all because, well . . because through your errors I learn to appreciate the *real* achievement of your contemporaries.

JACK

So why — continue? We both know you don't care one way or the other about a night in the sack. I even get the feeling you go that route out of some strange sense of obligation to your — your womanhood. Like you're trying, fighting, to keep your membership in that little club. As if you're afraid you don't really belong . . anymore. (*Norma deliberately pushes over the flower vase; water spills onto Jack's trousers. For a quick moment we sense he'll retaliate; instead, he breaks into a smile. She, having no glass, coffee, etc., with which to fidget, opens her purse, pulls out a cigarette, and lights up. Lita moves toward Wallace, who is sipping coffee. She arrives, holds. Pause. Presently, he looks up.*)

LITA

Don't you want me . . to sit? (*Slight pause. She sits. He continues with his coffee.*) I've seen you before. Haven't I? (*slight pause*)

WALLACE

No.

LITA

What time is it?

WALLACE

Time?

LITA

It's important to know the time. Don't you think? I mean, where would we be if we didn't know the time? A lot of people would be late . . for appointments. (*slight pause*) I've seen you someplace. I'm sure. Maybe not here, but some other place. Your face is familiar. I always remember a handsome face. They're so much prettier. (*He half smiles.*) You're sure now. I'm positive I've seen you . . someplace. (*pause*) What's in the case? (*He doesn't answer, sips coffee.*) I mean I haven't seen one as *big* as that, before . . in a place like this. What I mean is . . especially in a place like this. (*moves her chair close to him, starts to slide her hand over the case.*) What's in it? (*coquettishly*) Tell me. *Please.* (*slight pause*) Why not dance with me? The floor's empty, which means we'd have it all to ourselves. (*slight pause*) I dance well. In fact, I'm a great — a truly fine . . dancer. You'd enjoy me. (*He looks at her quickly, smiles perfunctorily, then back to his coffee.*) Well, some other time. (*She forces a smile, rises, walks to Linden who coldly stares at her. She sits. Astonished*) You ate all the

19

cheese! (*He smiles, pleased with himself.*) He ate all the cheese! (*Orlando's desk phone rings. Orlando turns off the music, attends to the phone. Stan leaves the kitchen, carrying his bucket as well as a small transistor radio. A flourish of music of the news program type comes from the portable. Orlando throws Stan a dirty look, but he's busy with the phone. Jack and Norma listen with interest; Wallace stares at his case. Stan moves through the club and exits into the vestibule; the radio news as well as the sound of bailing water is clearly discernible.*)

RADIO VOICE

. . so young ladies, don't forget to use IT. IT, for that bright, fresh, clean, clear, hard look. The look that wins. IT. And it was another chocked-full, jam-packed, action-filled day today, like so many recently. Sad, tonight's first item: A vicious crime, this one, perpetuated by a berserk butcher by the name of Morton Sidecut. Sidecut (five feet four, dark-haired, and with a cleft in his chin) cut and quartered four of his best customers after locking the mahogany front door of his establishment and posting a silver and black "Out to Lunch" sign. Shocked regular customers questioned after the incident testified to the fact that Sidecut was a robust, cheerful man who always had a joke for them, was kind to his pet cat, and who in every way was a normal and healthy adult American male. Mrs. Sidecut, on learning of the tragic incident, refused to believe it was her husband's doing, but when presented with color photographs admitted she was probably wrong. (*As Stan moves back into the club, Jack unsuccessfully attempts to catch his attention.*) News of the tragedy spread throughout the city, causing a drastic drop in meat sales which accurately reflect a day in which Wall Street experienced a fourteen-point decline in Dow Jones industrials. The drop elicited the following comment from a concerned individual: "Something will have to be done, or else." (*Jack succeeds in getting Stan's attention as Orlando finishes his phone conversation.*)

JACK

(*to Stan*) News doesn't sound too good tonight.

STAN

In the end, nothing works out. (*Orlando arrives at the table.*)

ORLANDO

Nonsense! Everything is always hunky-dory. It's all in how you look at it. Excuse us. (*pulls Stan aside; takes away his radio and turns it off*) I warned you never again to bring this thing out here! All it ever does is depress everyone. Full of distortions, propaganda. I myself refuse to listen to it! It's bad for business. Understand! (*Stan attempts to return to Jack and Norma, but Orlando collars him.*) And get those filthy galoshes off!

A GUN PLAY

(Stan nods, returns to Jack and Norma's table. Orlando moves to the vestibule, then offstage.)

JACK

Two Scotches, no water, two cubes of ice in each, *please*! *(slams the menus at Stan, who takes them and starts away)*

NORMA

Make mine a Bloody Mary. *(Stan exits into the kitchen. Wallace pulls a pipe and tobacco pouch from his jacket. He fills the pipe, lights up; satisfied, he puffs away. He turns his attention to the attaché case; with pipe in mouth he pulls it to him. He opens it, starts to check its contents — the audience can't see anything but hears a metallic sound. He's looking for something inside the case, but can't find it. He stands, forgets to close the case, walks to the pay phone, deposits a coin, dials. Pipe in mouth, he waits. He speaks — unheard — finishes, hangs up. Suddenly, extremely fatigued, he leans against the wall. Pause. With great effort, he stands straight and starts for his table. Lita rises quickly, moves to and intercepts Wallace. Pause. She takes out a cigarette. He takes it from her, lights it for her, returns it to her. She takes a long drag. Pause. Wallace pulls her into him and kisses her long and deeply. Linden moves to them. They pull apart.)*

LITA

(to Wallace) Have I introduced you to . . to . .

LINDEN

Linden.

LITA

Sometimes, I forget. I mean, there's so much to remember. *(to Wallace)* And your name is . . ?

WALLACE

Wallace.

LINDEN

Nice name. Sit down, won't you? *(They sit at Wallace's table.)* Known Lita long?

WALLACE

No.

LINDEN

No matter. To know her long is no more interesting than to know her not at all.

LITA

(to Wallace) Ha! Ha! Funny. I love a joke, don't you?

WALLACE

No. *(slight pause)*

21

LINDEN

Tell me Wal, what do you do for a living? (*Wallace rubs his brow, doesn't answer.*)

LITA

(*to Wallace*) Linden's in stocks, bonds, foreclosures, swindles. Things like that. (*slight pause*)

LINDEN

What do you do, Wal?

WALLACE

Nothing . . particular.

LINDEN

Oh wow . . wow.

LITA

(*to Linden*) That's the best kind of business. (*to Wallace*) Don't you agree? (*No answer. Pause.*)

LINDEN

(*rising*) Well, I certainly have enjoyed our little chat. (*They start for their table, but when they get there Linden remembers, moves to the phone, dials. We do not overhear his conversation. Lita sits. Orlando, who has reentered the club, is at his stand. Stan enters from the kitchen, tray in hand, heads for Orlando.*)

STAN

The cellar's flooding badly. The wine's going under.

ORLANDO

It's probably to be expected.

STAN

But the foundations! We could all go under!

ORLANDO

(*fatherly*) My boy, you worry too much about insignificant detail. Everyone knows it rains occasionally. That's the way things are.

STAN

But —?

ORLANDO

(*raging*) Enough buts! I refuse to be harangued by an employee! Don't ask questions! (*calmly*) What is, is. (*Stan moves to Jack and Norma, slams two Scotches down in front of Jack and gives Norma her Bloody Mary.*)

JACK

Listen — what's so wrong with occasionally being afraid?

NORMA

Occasionally.

JACK

Seems to me, if you do some thinking every now and then, it follows you've got to be a little afraid. Unthinking courage . . is not courage at all. It's instinct.

NORMA

Really.

JACK

And you — you're never afraid.

NORMA

Well . . one can't . . one shouldn't . . one mustn't be passive about these things. One should take a positive stand. One should be able to spot the danger signals and take action. (*sound of water being bailed*) *You* really must!

JACK

How?

NORMA

(*groping*) Involve yourself with . . with the things around you. With the world. Participate. (*slight pause*) *Go to the movies more often!* (*Stan starts for the kitchen, but is caught by Linden, who having finished his phone call gives the waiter some additional information regarding his order. Wallace places his case back on the table. Lita is finishing her wine as Linden returns.*)

LINDEN

Terrifying news.

LITA

What?

LINDEN

Market's dropped another five points, in Tokyo. It'll hit here soon.

LITA

Oh. Can you do anything?

LINDEN

What difference would it make. It wouldn't change anything. Things will get better. It *always* happens this way — first bad, then good.

LITA

But if it's dropping, isn't it going the opposite way — good to bad?

LINDEN

It's got to be bad before it can be good.

LITA

Oh.

LINDEN

If it were good and going to bad, I'd be in real trouble.

LITA

(*confused*) Then aren't you?

LINDEN

Six of one, half-dozen of another. (*pause*). In the meantime, I ought to invest in art. They're getting great prices today. It's a business. A real business. Always going up, never down.

LITA

You! Art? (*He turns toward Jack.*)

LINDEN

See that fellow. He's a very famous, maybe the most famous, *unsuccessful* painter in town.

LITA

(*interested*) Really! I don't think I know him. Do you?

LINDEN

No, but I know about him.

LITA

(*rising*) Let's dance. (*They rise and at first dance in close proximity, but are soon floating in opposite directions, each jerking and thumping to his own fantasy. During one section of the dance both find themselves facing a mirror: for a few moments each dances with his own image. But the music changes and they pull together again, dance a slow, casual number.*) What do you know about him?

LINDEN

I saw him at a party.

LITA

Whose party?

LINDEN

Amy's. (*She stops.*)

LITA

Why wasn't I there!

LINDEN

You were, with me.

LITA

Then why didn't you introduce me to him?

LINDEN

I told you — I don't know him! (*They resume dancing.*)

LITA

He's so . . interesting looking.

LINDEN

They always get the best looking girls, those types.

A GUN PLAY

LITA

From what he's got with him, I wouldn't say that's *necessarily* true.

LINDEN

(*dreamily*) Sometimes I think I should've continued with my photography. You know, in college, I was on the school paper. I took good pictures. No — I took *very* good pictures. Some might even say excellent ones. And today, who has a better life than a photographer. And . . maybe — maybe I . . could've . . Well anyway . . Oh well . . (*They continue dancing a few more beats, then Lita halts abruptly, glances at Jack.*)

LITA

What's his name?

LINDEN

Why?

LITA

Why not!

LINDEN

Jack, I think.

LITA

Nice name. (*They resume dancing.*)

LINDEN

Didn't that news report scare you?

LITA

Silly, of course not. I'm a big-city girl. I know life. I know things like that. It's always happening. Even now, something . . is happening, like that. One becomes used to the sadness of it all. Anyway, it'll all be on the late evening news.

LINDEN

Ever seen a dead person?

LITA

Naturally! In magazines and newspapers — on television. Ghastly! (*slight pause*) When I was a little girl, I went to my uncle's funeral. It was pretty. Flowers of all kinds: dandelions, roses, orchids, violets. All the colors of the rainbow.

LINDEN

(*to himself*) Yeah, I should've been a photographer.

LITA

Stop interrupting me! (*nicely*) Only last week I picked up a magazine. It had this exquisite article on "Crime in Our Time." Terrible pictures of the worst sort of . . things. But the photographer, whoever he was, was a consummate artist. He captured . . Linden! *Are you listening?* (*He nods.*)

Well, he captured each moment so beautifully that the subject matter — yes, the subject matter itself was, was transformed. Transfigured! The horrors were, in some strange way, made beautiful. Like the paintings of an Old Master. (*slight pause*)

LINDEN

(*innocently*) What was the point of the article?

LITA

Huh? Oh, I don't know! How could anyone remember? Don't be ridiculous! (*Jack and Norma rise, move onto the dance floor. They bump and grind in a more decidedly low-keyed manner than Lita and Linden. As both couples dance we hear, offstage, the sound of a motorcycle growling to a halt. The first motorcycle officer appears in the vestibule. He wears helmet, dark-lensed goggles, which he never removes, boots, tight jacket, etc. Strapped around his waist are two pistols; strapped around his shoulder, a small radio from which emanates an incomprehensible police call. Everyone keeps dancing though it's impossible not to hear the noise of the call or notice the officer. Wallace seems a bit uneasy. The officer holds in the vestibule. Calls continue. Orlando moves to the officer.*)

ORLANDO

May I be of any help, officer? (*The officer stares at him, says nothing.*) Could you . . do you think you might lower the radio? (*He switches it off.*) Could I interest you in a cup of coffee? (*The officer turns his back to Orlando.*) On the house, of course. (*no reply*) Our coffee is superb. (*no reply*) It's absolutely impossible to get a cup the equal of ours anywhere east (*correcting*) — west of Vienna. (*The officer starts into the club.*) At least tell me if it's raining outside! (*The officer starts to slowly circle the club, silently observing the dancers. Wallace glances at his open case. The officer is moving in an arc toward Wallace, but is not paying him particular attention. Wallace closes his case. He puts it beneath his table. The officer arrives at Wallace's table, towers over him, stares down. Wallace sips some water. Pause. Orlando turns off the dance music. Couples on the floor return to their tables, all staring at the officer who stares at Wallace. The officer resumes moving, giving the others a quick look-over before reaching the vestibule. He turns once again, surveys the club, exits.*)

NORMA

Brutal, those cops.

JACK

Define yourself.

NORMA

Define myself? Didn't you see how he terrorized this place? Not saying a word. Trying to scare us. Moving and checking. I tell you it was a *brutalizing* experience.

JACK

I didn't notice you do anything but dance. You certainly didn't look brutalized. Would you like to be? (*Jack lights a cigarette. Linden rises, exits into the men's room. Stan moves out of the kitchen, tray in hand, and heads for Orlando.*)

STAN

The cook wants a raise. (*hurries to Lita and after great difficulty uncorks a fresh bottle of wine*)

LITA

(*concerned*) Did you hurt yourself? (*Stan smiles, hurries back toward Orlando, who waits impatiently.*)

ORLANDO

Say that again. Slowly.

STAN

The cook wants a raise. *Now*, he says.

ORLANDO

How dare he!

STAN

He says, if he doesn't get a raise *now* — he'll wreck the kitchen.

ORLANDO

Oh, go on. He wouldn't.

STAN

All I'm telling you is what he told me.

ORLANDO

How do I know you're telling me what he told you?

STAN

Go back and ask him yourself!

ORLANDO

You know I can't do that. It's quite impossible. I've got a business to run. First things first! Now —

STAN

(*interrupts*) What about the cellar? It's in bad shape.

ORLANDO

There are some things one must, and you'd better learn this if you want to become a head waiter —

STAN

(*interrupts*) But I don't want to be a head waiter.

ORLANDO

(*stunned*) No??

STAN

(*proudly*) I want to be a maître d'. (*slight pause*)

ORLANDO

There are things one must push to the background, Stanley. That is, if one wants to move *up* in this world. To think of them would be enough . . enough to prevent . . Anyway, there are things, which are . . which are simply too . . (*Loses his train of thought; in addition, he's concerned that the customers will overhear and so modulates his voice.*) However, it's the . . the — Yes! (*energetically*) Stanley, where are the candelabras? The brass ones! They should be out, on top of the pastry stand. Get them! Get them immediately! (*Stan exits into the kitchen. Into the vestibule step George and Melinda. Orlando spots them.*) Arrivederci!

GEORGE

Hi!

MELINDA

(*simultaneously*) Hi! (*Orlando moves toward his new customers. Melinda smiles a contented and happy girl-next-door smile. George stands with the casual grace of a western hero. Both wear wet raincoats and carry umbrellas.*)

ORLANDO

A table no doubt.

GEORGE

Sure would appreciate one.

MELINDA

Oh yes, we would. Very much.

GEORGE

Another couple might join us later. I hope you don't mind.

ORLANDO

Most excellent. Then you'll be quatro en numero.

GEORGE

Oh yeah, swell! (*Orlando scours the room, zeros in on Wallace, who has pulled the case to him and is staring at it. Orlando motions the two to wait. He moves toward Wallace. Lita has focused all her attention on Melinda. As Orlando moves we hear a thunderous crash of pots and pans, accompanied by screaming in an undistinguishable foreign tongue. Orlando halts, sighs, pulls himself together, continues on. He reaches Wallace.*)

ORLANDO

Excuse me, commendatore. But would you mind my moving you to another table? A table more centrally, prominently, yet discreetly located. I'll have the waiter bring you a fresh pot of coffee, compliments of the establishment. (*Wallace nods his assent. Orlando picks up the coffee, etc., and moves him to a small table at center right. He then returns to Wallace's old table, using Wallace's linen napkin to wipe it clean. Heading back to the waiting couple, Orlando dumps the soiled napkin on Wallace's table.)* Merci. *(George and Melinda follow Orlando, who before returning to his stand hands them the club's menu. They sit. Silence. Wallace opens his case. The audience as yet can't see its contents. Lita, who has been staring at Melinda, rises, moves casually toward her. She passes her twice, then heads for the powder room, but does not enter. She holds outside, staring at Melinda. Linden remains inside the men's room. Wallace lights his pipe again, takes a few puffs, stares at the open case. Stan comes out of the kitchen. Orlando signals him to attend to George and Melinda. He moves to the couple's table.)*

STAN

Yes. *(Melinda notices his galoshes, but says nothing.)*

GEORGE

We'd like something — nice.

STAN

Yes.

GEORGE

What could you recommend that's . . nice?

STAN

Everything here is first rate. *(They inspect the menu.)*

GEORGE

(reading from the menu) How about some "Merci pour votre patronage"?

STAN

Sorry, but we're all out of that.

GEORGE

Oh . . *(slight pause)*

STAN

(starts away) I'll be in the kitchen.

MELINDA

Don't go —

STAN

(turning back) Yes? *(Melinda points a "potluck" finger at the menu. She checks where it's landed.)*

MELINDA

We'd like some caneton.

GEORGE

Yes, that's a nice choice. Two caneton.

STAN

(mildly hysterical) Caneton!

29

GEORGE

Yes.

STAN

(*hurriedly*) Two caneton. Wine?

MELINDA

Oh no —

GEORGE

Not us.

STAN

Good. (*takes the menus and rushes to Orlando; upset*) They want caneton rôti à l'alsacienne!

ORLANDO

(*to the couple, grandly*) One of my favorites!

STAN

But the cook's gone! The kitchen's a wreck!

ORLANDO

Well do something. Improvise.

STAN

What?!

ORLANDO

(*screams*) *Don't bother me with details!!* (*regains control*) And a fresh pot of coffee for the gentleman. (*Stan exits into the kitchen. Wallace takes a last puff on his pipe, puts it down. He reaches into his attaché case and pulls out the handle section of a three-sectioned machine gun. Next the chamber, and finally the barrel section. He starts to assemble the gun. No one in the club notices him: the two couples are engaged in conversation; Lita is staring at Melinda; Orlando is busy at his stand; Linden is in the men's room. Wallace completes assembling the machine gun — which is painted blue. He rises, slowly turns so that he is facing all the others in the club. He starts to lower the machine gun into firing position. Very long pause. Wallace and his gun have gone unnoticed. He swings it across the club. Finally, the weapon is pointed at Orlando who, a few moments after it fixes on him, looks up from his ledger, pulls back. Now all in the club notice Wallace; at the same time he again starts to swing the gun across the room. Jack and Norma observe casually: it's as though they were watching an absorbing movie, all somewhat remote. Melinda, as the gun is pointed at her, screams; but her terror is eased in light of her husband's seeming calm. Linden leaves the men's room, stands beside Lita, who is coolly viewing Wallace.*)

LINDEN

What's all this about?

A GUN PLAY

LITA

(*thrilled*) I don't know. (*Presently, Orlando, having regained his composure, moves toward Wallace. Wallace's attention is now fixed on Lita. She throws a seductive smile at him.*)

ORLANDO

(*sternly*) What's the meaning of this? Come now. I have a right to know! If I don't, who does? (*Wallace turns the gun on him; Orlando puts his hands up.*) What . . I repeat . . is the meaning of this? (*Wallace, visibly nervous, pulls the gun into his body, as if he is about to fire. Norma rises, moves slowly toward him. She holds in front of him. Pause. She gently rubs his forehead, takes the gun; he offers no resistance. Pause. Norma's face lights up as she turns, aims the weapon at Jack. She wraps her finger around the trigger, aims, but doesn't fire.*)

NORMA

(*gleefully*) Rat-atat-tat! Rat-atat-tat! Dead, you're dead. I killed you . . dead. (*slight pause*) Rat-atat-tat. (*Jack feigns being hit, then glares hatefully at her. She turns to Wallace.*) He's dead. (*Wallace sits. All seem relieved by this playacting.*)

MELINDA

Oh George — a game! A game! (*Stan leaves the kitchen, carrying a tray holding a pot of coffee. He moves toward Wallace as Lita grabs the gun from the table. Stan, who had not previously seen the weapon, is considerably shaken on seeing it. He barely manages to put down the coffeepot.*)

LITA

(*to Wallace*) Oowh! George Raft used one just like this last night — on the Late Show. He was marvelous. Didn't think twice about pulling the trigger — (*mugging*) Rubbing out a few. (*sadly*) His wasn't blue though. (*Lita, playing with the gun, aims toward the ceiling — and fires. Plaster and chalk sprinkle down. Excited*) It works! (*quickly fires another short burst*) It really works! It works — it really works! (*to Stan*) Did you see George Raft last night? He — (*Stan turns to Orlando.*)

STAN

(*to Orlando*) It fired! It fired real bullets!

ORLANDO

(*to Stan, hard*) What else should it fire! It's a gun, isn't it? (*sadly*) My beautiful ceiling. (*to Lita, taking the gun*) If you don't mind.

STAN

But it fired bullets!

ORLANDO

(*screams*) That's what guns are for! To fire bullets!

STAN

But —

ORLANDO

Everyone knows that!

STAN

But it —

ORLANDO

But me no buts! I'm warning you! (*points the gun at Stan*) I'm only human! I can be pushed so far, and no farther! (*Stan, terrified, backtracks.*) See! Gun! Gun is machine that fires. When it fires, it makes holes — in floors, walls, upholstery, linen — It fires by pulling trigger. (*points the gun at the ceiling*) Like this — (*Pulls the trigger: nothing. He's disappointed.*) Empty . . (*to Wallace*) Empty? (*no answer*) Everyone, be on guard for falling plaster. We wouldn't want anyone to get hurt. (*Orlando seems upset with the prospect of repairs. He returns the gun to Wallace who sets it down on the table. Wallace looks at the gun, checks his watch, looks for a wall clock. There is none. He pulls out his tobacco pouch, fills his pipe, and lights up. Orlando moves back to the stand.*)

MELINDA

George, it's all right now, isn't it?

GEORGE

Oh, I wouldn't . . worry about it. It's only an old army issue. Out of date though. The stuff they're using nowadays is much more efficient, less costly, easier to operate. Wonder who did the paint job? (*short pause*) If you want, I'll go take a look. Would you like that?

MELINDA

If you would, yes.

GEORGE

Sure. (*He rises.*)

MELINDA

George darling! (*He can't get away because she's holding his wrists.*) Don't offend the gentleman. It wouldn't be good manners.

GEORGE

Don't worry. I'll be quite correct. (*Chops her wrists. She lets go. He starts away.*) You know that. (*As he heads for Wallace, he's intercepted by Stan.*)

STAN

Sir, I'm afraid we're all out of the rôti for your caneton.

GEORGE

That's okay. My wife won't know the difference. (*They continue to talk though we don't overhear them. Lita rises and moves toward Melinda, ap-*

proaching her from behind. She touches Melinda's shoulder, her hand caressing the material.)

LITA

It's a smashing dress. I adore the material. Divine. Where can I get it? I must have it. Really, I must. I won't take no for an answer. (*Melinda's so tense she can't answer. Lita laughs, dashes into the powder room. George moves to Wallace, who is smoking.*)

GEORGE

Hi. (*Wallace looks up, nods.*) Eh, nice night . . tonight.

WALLACE

Yes.

GEORGE

(*indicating gun*) Mind if I take a look?

WALLACE

Help yourself. (*He picks up the gun, inspects it. He looks it over in a manner which demonstrates his familiarity with weapons.*)

GEORGE

Who did the paint job? (*silence*) You? (*silence*) Well, one thing you gotta admit, they sure knew how to build them in the old days. Solid, well constructed, did its job quickly and effectively. In a way we've lost the ability to make 'em like this today. Simplicity is out. Everything is complicated . . but we're the better for it. (*slight pause*) Still, in the old days . . they knew . . a few things too. Don't you think?

WALLACE

(*indicating gun*) You have something to do . . with —

GEORGE

No, not actually . . Not like this. But a long time ago, I might have.

WALLACE

What is it, you do, now? (*George stares at him for a moment, then breaks a big smile. He starts to explain, using his hands as though he were trying to construct the answer with them, rather than with words.*)

GEORGE

I . . I . . eh . . What I do is — (*embarrassed*) I . . eh . . I — Ha . . What I do is I build, rather I help to build — Ah well . . excuse me. I'm a space engineer. An aerospace engineer. A specialist in that area. It's a good job. Pays well. Room for advancement. It's a constant challenge, if you know what I mean. How about you? (*Wallace pours himself some coffee.*) What do you do? (*silence*) I bet you do something . . interesting. (*slight pause*) That's my wife over there. (*calling*) Honey — hi, honey. Hon-ey . . (*Punches the air, annoyed at not having been acknowledged.*

Pause.) Who . . did . . the paint job? (*Wallace slams down his coffee cup.*) Well, nice . . to have made your acquaintance. (*Wallace ignores him. As George starts for his table, Stan leaves the kitchen and moves to the maître d's stand.*)

STAN

You're not going to do *anything* about that gun?

ORLANDO

Absolutely not. For what reason? He's a customer, isn't he? So what if he's got that thing. Other customers bring in umbrellas, pocketbooks, dogs, cats, bad tempers, blotchy skin, bad manners, unrefined taste buds, filthy minds. And do we bother them? Do we? *Well, do we?* (*Stan, confused, moves off and back into the kitchen. George reaches his table, finds Melinda still quite flushed from the Lita experience.*)

GEORGE

Strange guy. Nice enough though, in his own funny way. Tight-lipped, but certainly that's his privilege. What's wrong, honey?

MELINDA

Oh, nothing . . Nothing.

GEORGE

Sure now? (*She nods "yes." Lita returns to her table, sits.*) You seem upset.

MELINDA

(*hysterically*) But I'm not! I'm not! I promise.

GEORGE

Well, if you say so, it must be. You're sure now? (*She nods "yes" again.*) All systems go? (*slight pause*) Last chance!

MELINDA

Well . . there is — *that* woman.

GEORGE

What woman?

MELINDA

(*afraid of drawing attention*) *No*, we can't talk about it.

GEORGE

Talk about what?

MELINDA

It simply wouldn't do. It wouldn't be polite, George. It wouldn't be nice. It's best to forget.

GEORGE

Forget *what*?!

MELINDA

I'm sorry. I can't talk. There's nothing wrong.

GEORGE

Well, if that's the way it has to be.

MELINDA

It does. Some things shouldn't be talked about. Some things are too upsetting.

GEORGE

But we're married. (*She bursts into tears.*) *I'm your husband.* (*to all*) I'm her . . husband.

MELINDA

(*still sobbing*) And I love you very much. Believe me I do. (*Stan leaves the kitchen, moves quickly to Orlando. He's wearing knee-length boots.*)

STAN

(*triumphantly*) Cats and dogs you've *never* allowed in!

ORLANDO

(*wearily*) I was merely making a point, Stanley. When one makes a point it can be made literally or figuratively, or as I am apt to do, both ways. Cats and dogs included.

STAN

But that man has a gun! (*slight pause*)

ORLANDO

Did you yourself not vouch for him? (*Stan nods "yes."*) And are you now not contradicting yourself? (*Stan nods "yes," then "no."*) And does not the old saying, first impressions . . first impressions . . Ah, yes, first impressions are best impressions, reassure you, as it does me, that there is absolutely nothing to worry about.

STAN

But don't you remember? When he came in, *you* didn't like him!

ORLANDO

Prove it! (*Orlando moves from behind the stand, glances at some of the customers who've overheard his outburst, pats Stan affectionately, fatherly.*) Take it easy. Don't worry so much. It takes all kinds to make . . a dull world. Ha! Ha! (*Stan starts for the kitchen, abruptly turns and returns to Orlando.*)

STAN

But that man has a gun! (*Wallace smokes his pipe, sips his coffee.*)

ORLANDO

Just look at him and tell me there's something to worry about. There he sits, nice and pleasant, smoking his pipe, bothering no one, enjoying our superb coffee. (*conspiratorially*) You and I know it's impossible to get a cup the equal of ours anywhere east . . I mean, west of Vienna, eh? So what if he's got a little something in that case of his? Has he done anything with it? Has he used it to hurt you, or me? (*Stan nods "no."*) Live and let live! That's what I say. Don't you? *Don't you!*

STAN

I guess you're right.

ORLANDO

Sure I am. It's better that way. Ah well, back to business. Everything okay in the kitchen?

STAN

It's a wreck.

ORLANDO

Too bad.

STAN

But how am I going to get their (*has trouble pronouncing it*) caneton rôti à l'alsacienne? The cook's gone!

ORLANDO

No problem whatsoever. Just get in there and get to work.

STAN

But I can't cook! You know that. Anyway, I'm a waiter.

ORLANDO

Stanley, this is a *golden* opportunity! It's your chance to prove what a fine restaura*teur* you are. An all-around type. You know, I'll be opening up another place soon. The demand for this sort of place is tremendous! I'll need a competent type to run it. A jack-of-all-trades. An all-around type.

STAN

But I can't — (*Orlando grabs Stan's arm, twisting it, pressuring him.*)

ORLANDO

I like that smile of yours. It's a healthy one. It's the sort that pleases customers, fits comfortably behind a maître d's stand. Mind you, I'd even go so far as to say it's a smile that reassures people. Yes, I'm sure of that. They'd like it. (*removes the pressure*) Now just go back there and put together the caneton. Whip it up, my boy! It won't be much trouble. A wing here, some orange sauce there, a little heat, and voilà! (*Stan exits into the kitchen. Orlando turns up the music. George and Melinda rise and dance slowly, self-consciously. Lita stares at Melinda.*)

LITA

(*contemptuously*) Well just look at that bitch.

LINDEN

(*glancing from Norma to Melinda*) *Which* one?

LITA

That one. I was only admiring her dress.

LINDEN

Oh.

LITA

She's trying to make me feel guilty. (*at Melinda*) But it won't work. Insipid —!

LINDEN

Kinda cute. (*Melinda quickly returns to the table, sits. George is momentarily abandoned on the floor — quickly returns to his table.*)

GEORGE

What was I doing wrong, honey? (*Pause. Lita spots Norma, rises, moves to her table, smiles seductively at Jack.*)

LITA

(*to Norma*) I knew I recognized you. You're Norma! Norma of *Trends* magazine.

NORMA

Yes.

LITA

You write that wonderful column, "Trivia."

NORMA

Yes.

LITA

I read you every month — twice during the holiday seasons . . when you have two issues. (*She darts a playful smile at Jack. He returns the smile.*) You're always so with it. In fact, I'd say your column is ahead of it. It's a pacesetter.

NORMA

Oh, I don't know if I'd go that far.

LITA

All my best friends read you. We couldn't get through a month without you. Your column guides our lives. You see, we're night people. (*slight pause*)

NORMA

You're putting me on.

LITA

(*hurt*) Oh no! Please don't think that. Not for a moment. You see, I'm involved. (*She glances at Jack who seems amused by this conversation.*)

NORMA

Well then, you understand. Trivia's what's happening — *here, now*, today. Many of the country's biggest and best minds are devoted to it. It's everywhere you go, in everything you see. It's *that* important. And my job, as I see it, is to make sure American women *get their share*. Why shouldn't they?

They deserve it. American women have a *duty* to know and *we* have the right to inform. That's what I say in next month's column. I have the proofs right here. (*as she takes them from her purse*) You know, you were right about people like me — we do lead, we have to. I mean, someone does. (*reads*) Now, I say, "American women have a duty to know and we have the right to inform. So in their interests, we set the standards, create the barriers, destroy any chances for contentment" — but not . . of course . . for true happiness. (*puts the column away*) That's the trick, you see — *true happiness*. And that's what I do. Show them how they can live, how they *should* live. How to be happy *and* involved. Why not? It's the way things are, should be . . must be. It's the best way. Anyway . . it's my way.

JACK

Whoopee! (*Lita nods approvingly. Linden rises.*)

LITA

Is he one of your artists?

JACK

I'm yours, not hers, for the asking. (*Lita sits.*)

NORMA

He says that to everyone.

JACK

(*to Lita*) The name is Jack. (*Lita glances nervously at Norma, doesn't want to offend her, but . .*)

LITA

Lita's mine. (*Linden reaches the table.*)

LINDEN

And Linden's mine.

LITA

Linden's my date . . tonight. He's a stockbroker.

NORMA

(*intrigued*) Really. A stockbroker. (*laughs*) Stocks-and-blondes.

LITA

(*sotto voce to Norma*) Essentially he's a daytime person trying to go nighttime.

NORMA

(*to Lita*) I understand. (*to Linden*) I can be very . . sympathetic. (*Lita eyes Jack who returns her gaze.*)

JACK

(*to Lita*) I'd love to paint you.

LITA

I'd love to be painted.

NORMA

(*to Linden*) You must make piles of money for yourself and . . people. Don't you?

LINDEN

(*embarrassed*) No, at least not all the time.

NORMA

(*glancing at Jack*) Honesty! So refreshing. (*to Linden*) You're a man of action. I can see. I can tell. I know.

JACK

(*to Linden*) I've tried, but somehow always failed . . *on the market* that is. Do you think . . maybe, you could help me?

LINDEN

Why not? There are areas I know you could help me in. Parties. The scene. You *are* Jack the painter, the fellow in all those magazines? (*Jack, embarrassed, looks to Norma, who throws him a devastating smirk.*)

JACK

I've been in a few.

LINDEN

Good! That's what I thought. We can be of service to each other. I know a little about you, about the type of life you lead. It's a little of what I'd like for myself. We could do a lot for each other. To tell the truth, as I was just saying to — (*glances at Lita*) to . .

LITA

(*horrified*) Lita!

LINDEN

I was just saying *to her* that I'm interested in starting an art collection. No reason why I can't start with one of your paintings. Buddy! You and I are going to get along great. (*Linden sits. Jack smiles, glances at Lita, turns back to Linden.*)

JACK

You may be right. I hope so.

LITA

(*to Norma*) Have you seen any of the work I've done? I'm in all the magazines, most of the time. (*slight pause*)

NORMA

What do you look like?

LITA

Look like?

NORMA

In the ads and magazines.

LITA

Oh . . Well, I've been everything. Blondes, brunettes, redheads. Fresh-cheeked young mothers in their "dream kitchens." Devastating types with that "I've been there before look."

NORMA

Déjà vu.

LITA

What —?

NORMA

Déjà vu, dear. French for "I've been there before, honey."

LITA

Oh — French! I had the most delicious (*delights in pronouncing it*) ragoûts à la nantua bonne femme at Ferdinand-de-Fleur the other evening. Enhanced by a superb Moulin-au-vent, soixante-quatre. (*Silence. Afraid she's mispronounced*) Famme . . ?

NORMA

Lovely. But you were saying . .

LITA

I had the most delicious ragoûts à la —

NORMA

(*cutting in*) No, *before* — you were saying . . (*slight pause*)

LITA

Oh . . I see. Well, I've also, mind you with only the finest photographers, done some n-u-d-e modeling.

MELINDA

(*overhearing*) *Nude!*

LITA

(*continuing*) On beaches, on sailboats, in rivers, in the desert, abandoned mine shafts, even in the snow. Everyone — even some of the truly famous — does it today. (*at Norma*) I mean, a beautiful body, *if you have one*, is like a work of art. (*to Jack*) Wouldn't you agree?

JACK

Wholeheartedly.

LITA

(*to Norma*) I've also had a small but significant part in a student film. (*stands*) And *I've done TV commercials*!

NORMA

Oh, my God — TV commercials!

LITA

My most famous one was where I took a shower . . soaped myself — here . . and there . . (*provocatively playacts soaping herself*) up and down . . in and out. I really had so little hidden. You could see, but you couldn't see. It was a masterpiece. They told me it sold millions of products (*sits*) I'm sure you've seen that one, or one of the others.

NORMA

No, I don't think I've seen you. But I'm sure *many* have. (*slight pause*)

JACK

You ought to drop over to the studio. We can discuss things more fully there. You can see some of my work, close up.

LITA and LINDEN

(*together*) I'd be delighted! (*Lita, furious, returns to her table.*)

LINDEN

(*moving off*) Yes, we should get to know each other. Why don't you give me your address, later.

JACK

Sure. (*Linden rejoins Lita at their table. Lights down. Suddenly, a spotlight darts to a model standing in the vestibule. It's as if she's materialized out of thin air. Orlando fiddles with his dials and we get the soft music that usually accompanies a fashion show. The model wears a short fur coat which she cuddles sensually to her body. In contrast to the painted ascetic look common to most models, she possesses a robust and healthy sexuality. She's not tall and angular, but curved and supple. Lights up dimly, but only enough so that all the customers can be observed. The spot follows the model as she moves through the club toward George and Melinda. Melinda touches the fur, giggles excitedly. The model does her turns at their table, moves to the Lita/Linden/Jack/Norma table. The model makes her turns. Jack watches, Linden is captivated, Lita is jealous, and Norma assesses the girl with cool, detached professionalism. The model moves to Wallace. Again she makes her turns, but holds in front of him slightly longer than at the other tables. She's also a bit more sensual with him. He stares: a faint smile creases his face. The model steps back, makes one final turn.*)

MODEL

Coat by Manzinni. The finest furs. One thousand four hundred and seventy-five dollars, not including tax. (*The model returns to the vestibule, removes the coat, and is now in a striking and very revealing mini-skirted evening dress. The model moves through the room, a repeat of her first foray. Finished, she again pulls back to center stage.*) Mini evening dress. By Verruchio. The best materials. Only three hundred and sixty-five dollars, tax included. (*The model returns to the vestibule, and removes her dress. She is now in a mini slip, a see-through affair that reveals her to be naked underneath.*)

MELINDA

George, it's suddenly very hot in here.

GEORGE

(*without taking his eyes off the model*) Oh . . (*The model moves through the room as before. Finally, at Wallace's table, she holds longer than at the other tables and longer than she'd done previously. Her enticing movements take her so close to him that she even, with a sweep of her arm, caresses his shoulder. Wallace slowly reaches out to touch her. Just as contact is about to be made, she artfully pulls away. His hand remains dangling in thin air. He looks at it, then her, then at the other customers who are now watching him. He quickly pulls his hand back. The model moves to center stage.*)

MODEL

Slip. The finest silk. By Jean Claude. Only eighty-five dollars, tax included. (*The model, instead of returning to the vestibule, moves slowly toward George and Melinda, sleeks past them. Next to the Lita group, finally to Wallace who sits tight, doesn't move, stares straight ahead. Pause. The model pulls back to center stage. The model removes her wig. She is totally bald. Melinda and George turn away. The others observe calmly. The model moves forward, slightly. The lights dim on all but her. Pause.*) Human hair. Available at Oscar's. Price . . to be determined. (*A spot cuts her off immediately. Complete darkness. Silence. Lights up quickly. Orlando, behind his stand, fiddles with the dials and some brassy music bounces into the club.*)

ORLANDO

Messieurs, mesdames, et mesdemoiselles, the club will, of course, be more than happy to provide information on any of the previously displayed items. All you need do is ask. Merci. (*George and Melinda breathe easily again. Orlando moves toward George and Melinda; as he nears them a thunderous crash of metal and glass emanates from the kitchen. Orlando shudders, but continues on.*) How's our young couple?

MELINDA

Starved!

GEORGE

Famished!

ORLANDO

Good, that's the best way to be. Forgive us, but the meal will take *slightly* longer than usual to prepare. Minor difficulties. (*sotto voce*) Union problems.

GEORGE

How long will it take, do you think?

ORLANDO

It takes a little while usually. It'll take slightly longer than that.

MELINDA

How long is that?

A GUN PLAY

ORLANDO

Slightly longer than usual.

GEORGE

How much longer is slightly than usual? (*slight pause*)

ORLANDO

Slightly.

GEORGE

Fine then. Thank you.

ORLANDO

Be assured your caneton will be well worth the waiting.

MELINDA

We believe you.

ORLANDO

I'll have your salads in uno momento. (*exits into the kitchen*)

GEORGE

I used to like him. (*Wallace, who had started to smoke his pipe after the model left, searches his pocket for change, doesn't find any, stands. Orlando, who has moved back into the club, doesn't notice him motioning as he disappears into the vestibule. Wallace puts the weapon back into the attaché case, leaves it on the table, not closing the latch. He glances at the phone, puts his pipe into his front pocket, and moves to Lita and Linden's table. At first they're unaware of his presence. As he's about to ask for change Linden speaks.*)

LINDEN

Excuse me . . but your pocket's on fire. (*Wallace checks his pocket which is indeed smoking, though not on fire. He pulls out the pipe, puts it in his mouth, brushes off his jacket, and moves off into the men's room. He stands at the sink, facing the mirror. However, he does not attempt to wash himself. He remains motionless, staring straight ahead into the mirror, his pipe resting on the sink. Norma has focused all her attention on the gun.*)

JACK

He's a bit of a strange one.

NORMA

Colorful though.

LINDEN

(*rising*) Just another eccentric.

LITA

(*to Linden, indignantly*) What would the world be without colorful eccentrics! (*follows him to Jack and Norma's table*)

LINDEN

Normal.

LITA

(*acidly*) How dull. You and your kind would take all the zip and zing out of life. Stockbroker!

LINDEN

(*raging*) *Why do you always try to hurt me!* (*Pause. Norma rises and moves to Wallace's table. She bends, picks up the machine gun, looks it over.*)

NORMA

Wait a minute, I think . . there's something here . .

JACK

Yes, a machine gun.

NORMA

Our spring issue. I can see it. It's right! Perfect! The center ten pages. A full-color spread. (*waves the gun*) "Gangsters I've known," or . . perhaps, "Mobsters Mourn." We get Robinson, Cagney, Raft, Duryea, Bogart — (*at Jack*) Jack-the-Ripper.

JACK

Jack-the-Ripper. Really. (*Lita stands, moves toward Norma. George and Melinda listen, confused but interested.*)

NORMA

Each carries a tommy gun, a pistol, a knife . . something that *looks* lethal. We can even use a backdrop from the thirties . . and the victims are our little models wearing the latest fashions. We might even shoot it . . build it around the general theme of a . . why not? — a funeral procession. Long luxurious maple coffins, lots of plushy red upholstery . . dramatic color changes . . unusual lighting effects, the models playing dead, the gangsters parading at their side.

LITA

(*to Norma*) Fantastic! I've simply got to be in one of those coffins. Promise me you'll put me in one.

NORMA

I will. (*to Lita, but mostly to herself*) Then again, it might prove too difficult to shoot. Too expensive. (*Lita is disappointed. Norma moves toward the seated Jack and Linden.*) But maybe we . . yes . . in order to properly display the garments — they really couldn't be seen in a conventional coffin — we'll have special ones constructed with . . cut-away sides . . (*Linden uses the moment to grab the gun from her. Jack watches. Linden turns, points the gun at Lita, pushes the barrel into her stomach.*)

LITA

Hey, that thing hurts! Linden — it hurts! (*Linden pushes her onto the dance floor. She's terrorized.*) No! No! Please don't. S-t-o-p! (*Screams. Linden takes careful aim. Norma's concentration is broken. She slowly focuses her attention on what's happening. Like Jack, she steps back.)*

LINDEN

(pulls trigger) Chu-chu-chu. Chu-chu-chu. Chu-chu-chu. *(Silence. Lita, astonished that nothing has happened, that no bullets were fired, relaxes slightly.)* Well, show us, show Norma, how it'll look . . in the magazine. *Die. Now!* *(Pause. Lita smiles nervously, proceeds to make an elaborate set of movements as she falls to the floor, "artfully" dead. Linden, Norma, and Jack move to where she lies. They form a semicircle around her body. Silence. All stare at the body. Wallace has stepped out of the men's room and watches. Near him is Stan's waiter's stand. Wallace takes a glass of water from it and slowly starts to drain it.)*

NORMA

(to herself) Yes, it'll work. *(slight pause)* I'm sure of that. *(Pause. Norma breaks the trio, silently returns to her table. Lita rises and follows. Linden returns the gun to the table, follows Lita. Jack picks up the gun, starts to inspect it. Wallace finishes with his water, moves slowly toward Jack, whose back is to him. Lita, Linden, and Norma watch. George and Melinda talk to each other. Wallace halts behind Jack, who is still unaware of his presence. Pause. He reaches out and gently places both hands on Jack's shoulders. Pause. Jack slowly squeezes around.)*

WALLACE

I'd like it please. *(Jack hands it over.)* Thank you.

JACK

Don't mention it. *(slight pause)* It's really a fine piece of metal. Make an excellent free-form sculpture . . mounted of course, and placed in a garden or courtyard. I'm sure it would stand up under all weather conditions. Even bad ones. Though we don't have much of that sort . . bad weather, in this part, too much any more. It's an intriguing design in its own right. *(slight pause)* Did you ever think of doing . . something, like that, with it?

WALLACE

Thank you.

JACK

No trouble. *(Jack starts for his table. Wallace holds, looks over the gun, checks his watch, and sits. He lifts the attaché case off the floor and slips the gun into it, without taking it apart, lets the lid fall over it, though this does not completely hide the butt of the gun. He returns the case to the floor.)*

LITA

(to Jack) For a second, I thought the two of you weren't going to get along.

JACK

(*argumentively*) Why!

LITA

Raft and Cagney never did.

JACK

Raft and Cagney?

LITA

On TV last night.

JACK

What the hell does that add up to! Did he say anything, do anything that would make you say what you did! Well, did he!

LITA

(*confused*) What did I say?

JACK

He's a fellow with a gun, that's all. (*sits*)

LITA

I didn't say a word against him. I mean, I spoke to him myself, before. Anyone could tell he's a real nice . . looking fellow. (*to Norma*) Don't you think so?

NORMA

Not particularly. But let's change the subject.

LITA

(*relieved*) Good! What can we talk about? (*Silence. All thinking. Then, slowly at first . .*)

LINDEN

Sports!

LITA

Fashions?

JACK

Problems of the artist in a society that doesn't deserve —

NORMA

(*interrupts*) We want to talk, dear, not think. Tonight, anyway. For a change. (*cheerily*) Personalities!

LITA

Trends and things?

NORMA

That's more like it.

MELINDA

(*brightly*) Recipes! (*Silence. They ignore her. Then they speak rapidly.*)

LITA

Parties!

A GUN PLAY

NORMA

Vacations!

LINDEN

Sex!

JACK, LITA, and NORMA

(*simultaneously*) Yes! (*silence*)

LINDEN

(*cautiously*) Life insurance . . I took out the most exciting double-indemnity policy the other day — my mother is the beneficiary. Of course . . my eldest sister . . is furious. She has three children . . the oldest . . is . . twelve . . (*silence*)

NORMA

Name-dropping.

JACK

Therapists I've — we've known.

LINDEN

Speak for yourself.

LITA

Gossip?

NORMA

(*elated*) Gossip! How lovely. (*slight pause*)

LITA

At the Ritz the other day . .

JACK

I tell you it was an achievement if ever I saw one.

LINDEN

Sailing up the river he said to me.

NORMA

In those circumstances, how is one to know? (*slight pause; rapidly*)

JACK

Hate!

LITA

Dispensable.

LINDEN

Don't really care for.

NORMA

Adore! (*Slight pause. All breathe deeply, then continue, laconically.*)

JACK

Tell me, what's the latest?

LITA

Never at Armondo's.

NORMA

The oldest, updated.

LINDEN

Now the locker room at the men's club is something to think about. (*Wallace turns and watches this group. There is no definable expression on his face. All breathe deeply again, then continue, rapidly.*)

JACK

Yes.

NORMA

Oh course.

LINDEN

Why not?

LITA

Maybe.

NORMA

*Un*acceptable! (*They now speak very rapidly.*)

LINDEN

Absolutely.

LITA

Without a doubt, but *never* at Armondo's.

NORMA

Never?

JACK

Why not?

LITA

Agree.

JACK

Agree.

LINDEN

Me too! (*Pause. The three wait for Norma. Pause. Wallace turns away, checks his watch. Suddenly, with building velocity and edgy enthusiasm they continue.*)

JACK

Tell me, what's the latest —

LITA

Never at Armondo's —

NORMA

The oldest, updated —

LINDEN

Now the locker room at the men's club is something to think about —

JACK

Yes —

NORMA

Of course —

LINDEN

Why not?

LITA

Maybe —

NORMA

*Un*acceptable —

LINDEN

Absolutely —

LITA

Without a doubt, but *never* at Armondo's —

NORMA

Never?

JACK

Why not?

LITA

Agree —

JACK

Agree —

LINDEN

Me too! (*pause*)

NORMA

All right. (*All breathe deeply; then together in one last effort they speak.*)

NORMA, JACK, LITA, and LINDEN

(*simultaneously*) Really really really. Really really really. Hah hah hah. Hah hah hah. Hm hm hm. Hm hm hm. (*As their "Really . . Hah . . Hm" tumbles into cascading laughter, Melinda starts to laugh; as the momentum of her laughter grows, that of the other four fades. They stop altogether, turn toward Melinda, who is by now hysterical. Suddenly, she hears the others' silence, abruptly cuts off. Silence. Orlando enters from the kitchen, nattily carrying two small salads and a salad bowl. He moves to George and Melinda, sets the two salads down with excessive flourish.*)

ORLANDO

(*triumphantly*) Voilà! Une salade Orlando! You are *the first* to taste. (*George and Melinda smile. Orlando hovers over the table, feigning a nonchalantness that fails to hide his obvious interest. George chews, stops, glances at Melinda, puts his fork down.*) Not good?

49

MELINDA
Darling —
GEORGE
(*reassuringly*) No . . very good.
ORLANDO
(*relieved*) Ah, of course.
GEORGE
We'd appreciate you taking them away.
ORLANDO
Take away — you said they were good!?
GEORGE
They are.
ORLANDO
Then why? (*Melinda waits for George.*)
GEORGE
They don't . . smell right.
ORLANDO
(*sniffing salad*) *Smell right!?* But . . but —
MELINDA
(*embarrassed the others will overhear*) Sssh — Don't be offended. It's not what you think. It's really quite simple. You see, George and I prefer —
GEORGE
Bland . .
MELINDA
Bland salads. We can't —
GEORGE
We won't —
MELINDA
Allow onions —
GEORGE
Garlic —
MELINDA
Garlic, spices — any strong seasoning or smells into our home or our systems.
GEORGE
You see, we decided long ago not to permit any impurities —
MELINDA
Impurities —
GEORGE
Of any sort into our —
MELINDA
Bodies.

A GUN PLAY

GEORGE

(*at Melinda*) *Systems!* (*to Orlando*) There are lots of things —

MELINDA

Dust in the air —

GEORGE

Carbon monoxide, fallout —

MELINDA

Gypsy moths . . *Smut!*

GEORGE

I'll tell it, honey!

MELINDA

(*meanly*) Sure, sweetie!

GEORGE

There are lots of things . . that one can't control. But when something *can* be done, we do it.

ORLANDO

I see.

MELINDA

(*combatively*) So don't you dare be offended. All we want are —

GEORGE and MELINDA

(*together*) Two bland salads. (*Orlando removes the salads.*)

MELINDA

I mean, you have to draw a line somewhere.

ORLANDO

Two bland salads. (*Orlando moves to the stand, adjusts the music: a peppery number blasts through the club. Linden rises, moves up behind Lita, caresses her neck in a gesture designed to get her up to dance. Lita acquiesces, but remains seated for a few additional moments. She eyes Jack, then rises. Orlando carries the two "unused" salads to Jack and Norma, places them on the table.*) Compliments of the house. (*Exits into the kitchen. Jack and Norma move onto the dance floor. The music grows more heated and sensual. It's obvious from the way in which Lita moves her body that she's attempting to excite Jack. The same is true — though in a more subdued manner — of Norma for Linden. The music grows extremely frantic during which the couples negotiate a smooth exchange of partners. Now it's Jack/Lita and Norma/Linden. The two "new" couples grind their bodies into each other. As the music and each couple's desires peak, Jack grabs Lita and eases her to the floor; Linden does the same with Norma.*)

MELINDA

George look! (*He glances at the intertwined bodies.*) George — don't look! (*Both turn away. Wallace watches with modulated interest, then checks his wristwatch. The lovemaking continues. A second motorcycle officer, dressed exactly like his compatriot, walks into the vestibule. He spots the lovers but pays no particular attention. He pulls out a small notebook, searches through its pages. Wallace tenses, darts a look below his table: the butt of his gun is visible. He lifts his water glass, drinks, controls himself admirably. The lovemaking continues. The officer looks up from his notebook: he's found what he's been searching for.*)

SECOND OFFICER

(*sharply*) Are there any young marrieds here? (*looks around suspiciously*) I said, are there any young marrieds here? (*George and Melinda look at each other, hesitate, then both raise their hands.*)

GEORGE

Over here, officer. (*The officer moves to them, passing the bodies of the lovemakers, who, after quickly glancing at him, go back to work.*)

SECOND OFFICER

You both young marrieds?

GEORGE

Yes, officer.

SECOND OFFICER

Let's see some identification? (*George nervously searches his pockets but can't find his wallet.*)

GEORGE

It's in my coat. (*starts to move*)

MELINDA

Never mind. I've got something, dear. (*From her purse she removes a folding plastic card holder, hands it to George, who takes it, lets it fall open; it's about two feet long. Both scramble through it for the right card.*)

GEORGE

(*handing it to the officer*) Here, this one should do.

SECOND OFFICER

Take it out please.

GEORGE

But, officer — it's laminated!

SECOND OFFICER

Take it out please.

GEORGE

Laminated!

SECOND OFFICER

Out! (*George bites into the plastic, pulls the card, hands it over.*) Sorry, but we have a job to do.

A GUN PLAY

MELINDA

We understand. (*The officer checks the card, returns it to George, then glances at the lovemakers.*)

SECOND OFFICER

(*to Melinda*) What about them — young marrieds?

MELINDA

Oh no, not them.

SECOND OFFICER

(*indicating Wallace*) And him — a young adult (*indicating lovemakers*) like them?

GEORGE

(*pointing at Wallace*) Officer, I think it wise to let you know that that fellow has a —

MELINDA

(*interrupts*) Oh, George darling — don't bother the officer. It isn't nice. Really, I'm surprised.

GEORGE

But, darling, that fellow has —

MELINDA

(*interrupts*) George! — good manners.

GEORGE

(*sitting*) Sorry, dear, you're right as usual. (*to the officer*) Thanks, officer. And take care, hear. (*The officer has ceased paying attention to George. He's been nervously darting his eyes in the direction of the men's room and moves toward it just as Stan, wearing waist-length boots and carrying his bucket, leaves the kitchen. He spots the four lovers on the floor, steps over them, moving toward the dials on the console control.*)

STAN

Oh no! We don't . . we have not — I'm sorry but we can't — (*turns the music off*) There are some things we simply do not permit . . on the premises. (*Exits into the kitchen. Immediately Lita gets out from under Jack. They stand. She, with no warning, smacks him hard across the face, returns to her own table, occupies herself with hair, face, lipstick, etc. Jack returns to his table. Norma rises, followed by Linden. She smacks him, starts for her table.*)

LINDEN

(*recovering*) How time flies when you're having fun. (*Orlando leaves the kitchen, wondering who turned the music off. He carries two salads to George and Melinda.*)

ORLANDO

Two *bland* salads. (*Orlando returns to his console. Norma sits, lovingly reaches across to Jack who kisses her hand. Lita offers her cheek to Linden, who kisses it politely.)*

LINDEN

Hungry?

LITA

Mmmm.

LINDEN

(*calling*) Armondo! — I mean, Hernando. (*to Lita*) Sorry. (*calling*) Orlando! S'il vous plait, Orlando. (*Orlando rushes over.*)

ORLANDO

Oui, Monsieur Linden.

LINDEN

We'll have stroganoff and a bottle of Château Moulin-des-Artistes '65. The wine immediately.

ORLANDO

But '65 was not a year, how shall I put it, to remember. Might I suggest a *delicate* bottle of Château Maison?

LINDEN

No.

LITA

Yes.

ORLANDO

(*to Linden, sympathetically*) C'est la vie. (*signals Stan and moves to him*) Two stroganoffs and a bottle of *Château Maison!* Wine immediately.

STAN

(*weakly*) Stroganoff, two. Château — But the wine cellar. It's almost completely flooded. *I'll drown!*

ORLANDO

(*to Lita and Linden, laughing it off*) Nonsense! As you can see, he has a most excellent set of boots. (*to Stan*) No! (*sotto voce*) I thought this problem was settled. Remember my plans, your future. (*slight pause*)

STAN

Château Maison . . (*starts for the kitchen*)

ORLANDO

And two stroganoffs! (*Stan halts.*)

STAN

Couldn't they try some caneton? I have enough —

ORLANDO

No! (*He returns to his stand. Stan exits into the kitchen.*)

JACK

What's that?

A GUN PLAY

NORMA

A note to our accounting department about you.

JACK

About what?

NORMA

Your first one-man show, in quite some time. Here, look at the instructions, the price. (*Hands him the slip of paper; he doesn't check it.*) You've sold out . . every canvas.

JACK

But you know I haven't worked much. I don't have enough for a show.

NORMA

You'll paint them quickly.

JACK

I need time —

NORMA

You've got two months. That's more than enough time. We've got a deadline to meet.

JACK

Deadline?

NORMA

I haven't told you, have I? I've been saving it. A sort of surprise. We, the magazine, bought a gallery. It's an excellent investment, we think. Besides, it can always be used for parties.

JACK

But what's that got to do with me!

NORMA

And I persuaded the necessary people to launch the gallery with your one-man show . . to start the spring season.

JACK

Stop it, Norma.

NORMA

That's precisely *the sort of event* we need, to shoot our summer issue around.

JACK

(*stands*) *Stop it!*

NORMA

(*stands*) A show . . that's "The Talk of the Town." (*pause*) You do understand . . what we want. What I want. (*pause*) I'm sure you'll do a fine job. You haven't even looked at the price. (*He looks.*) It's more than generous, wouldn't you say? (*pause*)

JACK

More. (*A pretty young girl, wrapped tightly into a trench coat, walks into the vestibule. Orlando moves to her, and after consulting with her, points to Wallace. As she moves toward him, the second officer leaves the men's room, only now he's dressed like a Hell's Angel type. He carries a small bag into which he's put the parts of his uniform that do not fit his current persona; however, most of his police uniform, with only a few minor modifications, serves extremely well. Because of his sun goggles we never see his face. He exits through the vestibule. The young girl halts beside Wallace. Pause.)*

GIRL

Hi. (*Wallace nods, takes the pipe from his mouth, places it in the ashtray.*) Sorry to be so late. (*He nods.*) Here they are. (*From both coat pockets she pulls a few small boxes wrapped in brown paper. He takes them.*) Shall we charge them to your account? (*He nods. She pulls out a small credit-card machine, the type that imprints the card on a tear-sheet bill. He hands her his card; she imprints it, gives it back to him. He signs the bill; she rips off his copy and gives it to him.*) 'Bye now. (*As she exits, she glances at the club and its customers. Wallace stares at the packages, rips open one: it contains a clip of bullets. Stan slams through the kitchen door, carrying a tray with two glasses and a wine bottle. He wears fisherman's long boots; his entire body is soaking wet. Stan moves to Lita and Linden, uncorks the soaked red-wine bottle with ease — the cork's so loose it almost slips out, this in contrast to the waiter's previous battles with the cork. He pours. Linden elaborately inspects the muddied glass, sips with obvious hesitation, coughs.*)

LINDEN

(*recovering*) Excellent . . wine . . Stan. (*Wallace signals Stan.*)

WALLACE

I like . . I always have liked . . a little drink, before. I prefer everything to be in order. To be in place. (*lifts the coffeepot, starts to hand it to Stan*) Please. It's empty. Take it away. (*Reaching across the table, Wallace lets the pot fall before Stan can grasp it. It smashes to bits. Pause. Wallace starts to hand the cup and saucer to Stan, but this time the waiter takes them from him. Stan starts to bend in order to pick up the pieces. Wallace speaks good-humoredly.*) Don't bother. It was empty. No need to worry. There was nothing there, anymore. All gone. (*slight pause*) Anyway, I like things to be in order. (*Shuffles the remaining objects on his table; each is put into place.*) Don't you? (*Stan nods.*) I'm glad. You ought to dry your clothes. They're wet, you know. You could catch cold. And it's not worth it. Not at all. Bring me a Benedictine. Water too. Will you? (*slight pause*) You will, won't you! Thanks. (*Stan nods "yes," turns, glances at*

Orlando and exits into the kitchen. Silence. Suddenly, the following conversations begin, overlapping and intertwining during their duration.)

GEORGE

Salad was nice.

MELINDA

Yes it was.

GEORGE

Maybe the meal will be too.

MELINDA

Good manners.

GEORGE

I wouldn't worry about it.

MELINDA

It's all right now.

GEORGE

I wouldn't worry about it.

MELINDA

Good manners.

GEORGE

It's all right now. Still, I wonder who did the paint job?

NORMA

Don't we want to eat.

JACK

I don't.

NORMA

You're not upset?

JACK

What I get, I deserve. So will you.

LINDEN

Do you prefer your stroganoff with noodles or rice?

LITA

Rice of course.

LINDEN

Shouldn't we have told him — Orlando, I mean?

LITA

The menu says rice.

NORMA

Try to be kind *(slight pause)*

JACK

Why?

GEORGE
Yes, I wonder who did it.

MELINDA
Did what, darling?

GEORGE
The paint job.

MELINDA
You might ask.

GEORGE
I did. Strange guy.

MELINDA
Good manners.

GEORGE
You seem upset.

MELINDA
I'm sorry. Forgive me.

GEORGE
For what?

MELINDA
Being upset!

JACK
Place is jammed, isn't it?

NORMA
Not really.

JACK
Place is jammed, *isn't it?*

NORMA
Not really.

JACK
Isn't it!

NORMA
Yes, yes —

LINDEN
You know, I like this place. It's comfortable.

LITA
Plenty of people here now, including us.

LINDEN
What I like about this place is just that.

LITA
Pam, Amy, Gloria.

A GUN PLAY

LINDEN

I took good pictures. And today . .

LITA

Gloria, Amy, Pam.

LINDEN

What we're having is a late dinner. Supper, actually.

LITA

It's important to know the time. What time is it?

LINDEN

Supper time.

LITA

Bon soir. Bon soir. Bon appétit.

LINDEN

Merci . . bien. Bien merci!

LITA

It's a beautiful experience.

LINDEN

A bartender, waiter, maître d'.

LITA

All you had to do was ask. I mean there's so much to remember.

GEORGE

You dance so well. You always have.

MELINDA

Think so?

GEORGE

Yes.

MELINDA

Dinner will be just fine.

GEORGE

Yes. (*slight pause*)

MELINDA

You have to draw the line somewhere. (*pause*)

NORMA

You'll take me home —? (*pause*)

JACK

News didn't sound so good tonight. (*pause*)

NORMA

You'll take me home? (pause)

JACK

It's instinct — or is it habit?

NORMA

You *will* take me home . . ?

JACK

Don't mention it! (*slight pause*)

NORMA

Why don't we have dinner. I'm famished.

JACK

I'm not hungry.

NORMA

Oh.

JACK

Are you? (*slight pause*)

NORMA

No.

LINDEN

Stroganoff will go well with this wine.

LITA

It's the other way 'round. *This* wine with *that* stroganoff.

LINDEN

Six of one, half-dozen of another. (*Silence. Orlando claps his hands.*)

ORLANDO

And now, as it is nightly, it's time for our private collection of horror films. Tonight, a special treat! A compilation of favorite scenes from the club's collection. We have worked diligently to put it all together. And I'm sure all will enjoy the results of that effort. (*Polite applause from all — Lita more heatedly than the others — except Wallace. Stan leaves the kitchen carrying small bowls of popcorn which he deposits with the word "Popcorn" on each table before disappearing back into the kitchen. Orlando presses a button and a screen appears. The lights dim. The movie starts. It's a mélange of early horror films — preferably expressionist German classics like* Nosferatu *and* Caligari, *plus, perhaps,* Frankenstein, Dr. Jekyll and Mr. Hyde, The Mummy's Hand, *etc. Plenty of blood, death, strangulations, beheadings, vampires, etc. General amusement and ad libs from the viewers — even, perhaps, a few screams. But mostly, fun. A few minutes into the film, a sequence flashes across the screen which is not conventional horror footage, but documentary material taken at a concentration camp. In it are some prominent shots of female guards, who wear the long skirts and blouses common to their trade.*)

LITA

What neat outfits! I've got to have one. (*general confusion among the viewers*)

A GUN PLAY

LINDEN

It's a concentration camp.

JACK

A concentration camp?

LITA

Oh . . It's not so bad.

MELINDA

George, I really don't know why they're still showing that sort of thing. What good does it do?

GEORGE

No good, I guess. (*Along with these new pictures the music has changed to loud Nazi marching songs. Orlando, who has been at his desk, rushes to the center of the club, spots the new footage.*)

ORLANDO

What's going on here? What's happened —! (*He rushes to his desk, presses a button: the screen disappears, lights come up.*) Ladies and gentlemen, messieurs et mesdames — I'm mortally embarrassed. Please accept my apologies. Those pictures belong to another collection. A mistake at the laboratory, no doubt. By tomorrow night all will be well again. Thank you. (*He turns up the music. Lita rises and rushes to him.*)

LITA

I've got to see it again. I must! Those skirts!

ORLANDO

Excuse —?

LITA

The skirts! The ones those women wore . . with all the sad-looking people in the background.

ORLANDO

You wish to see that, again?

LITA

I must! Please! (*pause*)

ORLANDO

Tomorrow. Come by in the afternoon. I'll see what I can do.

LITA

Do try. It's important. (*Returns to her table. Stan leaves the kitchen, carrying a tray with two coffees and a Benedictine and water.*)

STAN

(*to George*) Coffee, sir. (*serves*)

GEORGE

But we didn't order coffee! We're *waiting* for our food.

STAN

I know.

GEORGE

Where is it!

STAN

It's being prepared.

GEORGE

(*annoyed*) What does *that* mean!

STAN

It's cooking.

GEORGE

You *are* making it!

STAN

Of course! But it's a very difficult meal to prepare! Don't worry, it'll be ready soon.

GEORGE

Don't you talk to me like that!

STAN

It's being prepared! (*slight pause*)

GEORGE

(*rising slowly*) I hate you. I hate you! I HATE YOU! (*Melinda grabs him, comforts him.*)

MELINDA

(*soothingly*) Caneton will come, caneton will come, caneton will come . . (*Stan pulls himself together, moves to Wallace, places the Benedictine and water on the table. Wallace takes the water, gulps it down greedily.*)

STAN

Is there something wrong? (*Wallace puts the glass down.*)

WALLACE

No, nothing.

STAN

You sure? I could help.

WALLACE

(*nicely*) Who can you help? Me. You. (*looking at others*) Them. (*looking at Orlando*) Him. (*slight pause*) Why should you? Nothing's wrong. All goes well. Why, just look at me. Take a good look. (*Stan is embarrassed.*) Why should I need help! (*slight pause; nicely*) Now don't get me wrong. I appreciate your offer, your kindness, your concern. Very thoughtful. What I'm saying, to you . . is simply, for discussion's sake. Why should *I* need help! Just look at me. I've got fine posture, good teeth . . I am handsome. And don't think that by admitting it, I'm conceited or stuck-up. I'm not.

I'm honest in these matters. People have been telling me how . . nice looking
. . I am . . since I was . . a child. That was long ago, naturally. (*Stan
nods with sympathy.*) But I never let it do the work for me, the good looks.
(*slight pause*) I worked. I studied. I sweated. Hear me! (*calmly*) As a result,
I'm what I wanted to be . . I'm . . I don't travel much. I prefer to take
little walks and sit in places, places that I know, have a quiet cup of coffee.
Not bother anyone — (*He opens the attaché case, removes the gun, jams
the bullet clip into it. Stan steps back, but he's been so overcome by Wallace
that he moves forward again. Wallace places the loaded gun on the table.
Diplomatically*) No, I appreciate your asking, but I don't need help. You
do, though . . I think.

    STAN

Excuse me?

    WALLACE

Forgive the personal comment. I don't think it's serious. I wouldn't worry
if I were you. (*lowers the empty attaché case to the floor, starts to rearrange
his table*) I like order . . form . . neatness. (*sips at the Benedictine*) I
always finish my drink. Why shouldn't I? I did order it. (*slight pause*)
Then . . when I'm finished . . everything is, one. (*He sips again.*) Fine
stuff. Good body to it. Solid. (*Stan nods, turns, exits into the kitchen. Music
comes up. Linden takes Lita's hand and they rise and dance, this time paying
loving attention to each other. Wallace rises, gun in hand. He faces the
dance floor. All spot him but no one views the situation with urgent alarm.
Melinda, however, does reach for her husband's hand. Wallace turns to
the wall — audience — with the gun under his arm. His face is expression-
less. Suddenly — with a spasticlike movement — he violently swings the gun
across the wall, spraying burst after burst of machine-gun fire. Sound of
crumbling plaster and shattering mirror. Lita and Linden stop dancing, stare
at Wallace. Norma and Jack watch passively; finally, she removes a small
Minox from her purse and snaps a few shots of Wallace. Orlando observes
Wallace with shocked interest. The firing stops. George rushes for Wallace,
who turns the gun on him.*)

    GEORGE

(*nervously*) Good . . shooting. But shouldn't you point that . . at . .
someone else — (*Wallace turns away. Lita rushes toward him.*)

    LITA

(*annoyed*) Please, not so loud next time. My eardrums! (*Orlando moves
to him.*)

    ORLANDO

(*indicating the wall*) My good man, there are limits to what Orlando will
permit! Everyone knows I'm more than open-minded. No one can challenge

that. (*Wallace points the gun at him.*) But . . but — why couldn't you have made a nicer pattern?

NORMA

On the contrary, I think he's done excellent work. It may seem wild, abstract, but beneath it one detects a delicate yet monumental consciousness at work. And what it gives us is a . . subtle pattern. (*starts to shoot pictures of the wall with her Minox*)

LITA

Yes.

GEORGE

She's right.

ORLANDO

(*pondering*) Hmm . .

MELINDA

Oh yes — it's pretty. Pretty . .

JACK

Bullshit! (*Pause. Norma glances at Jack, then returns to her picture taking. Wallace watches them.*)

ORLANDO

Yes. I see. I understand. (*to Wallace*) Thank you. You have given my club more . . more character. As well as a work of art. (*to Lita and George*) You know, when you think about it, this gentleman has bestowed a unique distinction on my humble place. What club can offer walls containing real bullet holes. Not since prohibition days! We'll have to turn customers away! (*to Wallace*) Care to . . try again?

GEORGE

Sure, try again. (*All, with the exception of Stan, urge him on. Pause. Wallace turns away, returns to his table, sits.*)

MELINDA

(*simultaneously with three succeeding speeches*) George, it's all over. Sit down.

LINDEN

(*simultaneously*) Too bad.

LITA

(*simultaneously*) Another time.

NORMA

(*simultaneously*) Doesn't want to play anymore. (*General disappointment as those who urged him on return to their tables. Orlando, however, still waits; finally, left alone — turning from Wallace to the wall — he returns to his stand. Wallace gulps down the rest of his water, places the gun in his lap. He again rearranges his table setting. From inside his suit jacket*) *he pulls a pair of steel-rimmed spectacles, puts them on. He lights up his pipe, puffs away. He raises his snifter of Benedictine, letting the overhead light filter through it: there is not much liqueur left. He sips while surveying the room. He glances down at his gun, looks up, puffs on his pipe. There is the sound of a door opening and closing. Johnni, a young boy of eight or nine, dressed in the sort of outfit common to private schools — i.e., shorts, cap, knee-length socks, etc. — enters the vestibule.)*

JOHNNI

Where's my mummy?

ORLANDO

What's the meaning of this? Who are you and what's your name?

JOHNNI

My mummy told . . to meet her . . *(He starts to cry.)*

ORLANDO

(consolingly) Oh now now. Nothing to cry over, young man. We've got to be adults. *(pats Johnni sympathetically)* But you really can't stay here. It's much too late. You should be in bed.

JOHNNI

My mummy said to meet her here.

ORLANDO

Who *is* your mommy?

JOHNNI

*Mom*my?? *(starts to cry again)* My mummy.

ORLANDO

Young man, I'm afraid you'll have to leave. I will not risk violating the minors' law. *(Melinda rises, moves to Johnni.)*

MELINDA

(to Johnni) Don't cry. Mummy will come. *(to Orlando)* He can sit with us. *(George rises.)*

ORLANDO

Only until his mother comes. *(George drops a silver quarter into his palm. He stares at his "tip," dumbfounded.)* There are laws, you know . .

MELINDA

Come. Mummy will be here soon. *(They return to their table, sit.)* What's your name?

JOHNNI

Johnni.

GEORGE

Nice name. *(Stan leaves the kitchen, drenched and still in long boots.)*

MELINDA

And what grade are you in?

GEORGE

Play football?

JOHNNI

Yes.

GEORGE

How about golf?

MELINDA

(*admonishingly*) George! (*Stan arrives with the couple's meal, surprised to see the child.*)

STAN

Your caneton.

MELINDA

(*to Johnni*) Look at the nice caneton.

STAN

(*sotto voce*) I wouldn't give any to the kid. (*starts off*)

GEORGE

Could we trouble you for a glass of milk?

STAN

(*turning back to them*) Why not! (*turns away and moves to Jack and Norma; picks up their coffee cups*)

JACK

Two Scotches. (*Stan nods, starts away.*)

NORMA

And a Bloody Mary. (*He continues to Lita and Linden, checks their table; nothing is needed.*)

LINDEN

Fine wine, Stan. (*Stan continues toward Wallace. Lita pulls out her pocket mirror, once again begins her ritual. Stan stops at Wallace's table, stares at the bullet holes in the wall.*)

STAN

Anything else? (*Wallace holds the Benedictine glass up to the light. There is only a drop left.*)

WALLACE

No, nothing . . more. I'm about — finished. (*Wallace lowers his Benedictine, hands the empty water glass to Stan. Stan takes it, glances at the bullet holes again, is about to say something, but changes his mind. He exits into the kitchen. Wallace finishes his Benedictine. He lifts the glass to the light to make sure it's empty. It is. Yet he once again attempts to drain it. He pulls a handkerchief from his jacket, takes off his glasses, lifts them to the light, wipes them, puts them back on. He then uses the handkerchief to wipe the Benedictine glass clean. He places the glass neatly*)

66

on the table, setting it directly between the fork and knife. Wallace picks up his pipe, takes one last puff, puts it in the ashtray. He loads a fresh clip of ammunition into his gun. The music peters out, is replaced by a low electronic buzz. Everyone onstage is engaged in his own activity: Orlando at his ledger; Lita with her mirror and Linden watching her; George and Melinda eating and smiling at Johnni; Jack and Norma confronting each other. Wallace rises. He faces the occupied tables, pulling the gun into a firing position. Pause. Norma notices him, stands, pulls out her Minox, starts to snap pictures. She stops, smiles, laughs. Her laugh attracts the others' attention. One by one they turn to Wallace, seem amused, expectant.)

MELINDA

(to Johnni) Put your hands over your ears, dear. You too, George. *(George, Melinda, and Johnni turn away from Wallace, hands over ears, waiting for the inevitable noise. Norma snaps another picture, then stops abruptly. Linden, Lita, Jack, and Orlando turn from her to Wallace. Norma's smile disappears. Complete silence.)*

NORMA

(screams) No! No! NOOOooooo — *(Wallace, calmly and coolly and methodically, sprays the room with death. Silence. Without checking the bodies, Wallace returns to his table, picks up his attaché case, calmly takes apart his gun, and packs it away. He surveys the room, removes his glasses, cleans them, puts them away. He rises, starts for the door, carrying his attaché case; suddenly, he stops, returns to the table, picks up his pipe, cleans it out, puts it in his breast pocket. He starts up the stairs as Stan moves out of the kitchen, carrying a tray holding a glass of milk. Wallace halts, turns. Stan's and Wallace's eyes meet. Silence. Wallace turns away and exits through the vestibule. Dazedly, Stan glances across the carnage, then with great self-control places the glass of milk on one of the tables. There is the sound of running water. Soon, from behind the kitchen door, water starts to flood into the club. Stan notices the water, turns away from it. He drops his tray, holds in place, dazed, drained . . Static from the club's music system singes the air. Soon it fades, replaced by light, frivolous music.)*

THE END

67

A Gun Play by Yale M. Udoff was presented January 8–
February 14, 1971, by the Hartford Stage Company, Hartford, Connecticut. It was directed by Paul Weidner.

Cast of Characters

STAN	David O. Petersen
ORLANDO	Henry Thomas
WALLACE	Ted Graeber
LITA	Charlotte Moore
LINDEN	Robert Moberly
JACK	James Valentine
NORMA	Darthy Blair
FIRST MOTORCYCLE OFFICER	James Carruthers
GEORGE	Ron Frazier
MELINDA	Tana Hicken
FASHION MODEL	Dolores Brown
SECOND MOTORCYCLE OFFICER	Christopher Andrews
YOUNG GIRL	Robin Murphy
JOHNNI	Michael Esterson

The New York City production opened October 24, 1971,
at the Cherry Lane Theatre. It was directed by Gene Frankel.

Cast of Characters

STAN	Eugene Troobnick
ORLANDO	Arny Freeman
WALLACE	Tony Musante
LITA	Lara Parker
LINDEN	William Bogert
JACK	Jim Weston
NORMA	M'el Dowd
FIRST MOTORCYCLE OFFICER	John Doherty
GEORGE	Robert Moberly
MELINDA	Kelly Wood
FASHION MODEL	Pat Evans
SECOND MOTORCYCLE OFFICER	Ralph Maurer
YOUNG GIRL	Cheryl Houser
JOHNNI	Shane Ousey

ALLEN JOSEPH

Anniversary on Weedy Hill

to Terry

Cast of Characters

SETH HAGEN
VIRGINIA
MINNIE SKINNY
LEFTOVER EATER
CRANBERRY JUICE

ANNIVERSARY ON WEEDY HILL

It is 4:30 P. M. in the Bunker Hill district of downtown Los Angeles, overlooking one of its many freeways. A weedy hill is the outdoor home of Seth Hagen, a bearded, fifty-two-year-old derelict. An old, no longer used billboard stands upper right stage, with some faded lettering on its peeling front. A ladder leans against it. Seth has nailed some crates to the billboard to house garden tools, a few magazines, and other items. The shelf of the billboard contains more of his meager possessions, including mail. Down right we see a small vegetable garden. Slightly above it are a couple of boxes which make up Seth's workbench. A battered wind-up toy soldier which walks and a small telescope or pair of binoculars rest on one of the boxes. A tree stump lies center. An ancient sewing machine is outlined against a wide cyclorama on the crest of the hill. Down left stage is a worn automobile seat, which serves as a couch. Prominently displayed is a red hammock, with one end tied to the billboard and the down-stage end to a metal stanchion weighted with sandbags and rags. Far upper right are a small palm tree and bushes. The predominant colors are green and brown with splashes of red and yellow. As the play progresses the lights on the sky and the set should change toward a glowing sunset and twilight. Virginia, in a ragged nightgown, is dozing on the car seat. Seth is tending to his garden down right, occasionally pulling out a radish and eating it. We hear the distant drone of the freeway traffic located somewhere in the audience. Suddenly a rat scampers out of an old box of crackers lying on the ground. Seth leaps up and playfully stomps after the disappearing rodent.

SETH

Leave some for me, piker. What ya come stealin' from me when I got my back turned? (*throws a handful of crackers uphill*) Up somebody else's

71

leg, ya twitchy squeaks. (*Virginia wakes up and stares out at the audience. She is a worn-out, middle-aged woman with long hair. She has a vague quality highlighted by short bursts of energy. Her mind slips in and out of the past.*)

VIRGINIA

That rush hour traffic gets worse every day.

SETH

(*finding a cigarette in a torn coat that has been lying on a rock*) Hot damn! Lookit that. A whole smoke intact.

VIRGINIA

All that rumpus on the freeway and you flailin' at the rats —

SETH

(*searching for a match*) They my pets, Miss Virginia. Some people like dogs, cats, birds, little fishes. I find kinship with rats. But some of them been filchin' behind my back lately. Must be some new ones who ain't learnt the rules yet. (*coughs*) Gotta match, Ginny?

VIRGINIA

No.

SETH

Shi-et.

VIRGINIA

You know I don't smoke, Mr. Hagen.

SETH

(*sitting at the workbench*) Yeh, I know you don't smoke, Miss Virginia.

VIRGINIA

I used to smoke.

SETH

Yeh, and you give it up. (*picking up the toy soldier and addressing it*) God-damn, here I sit with an intack smoke and no match. (*Having wound up the toy, he sets it on the ground and crawls along with it as it marches toward the tree stump.*)

Riga digdigdig, riga digdig — soldier boy, soldier boy,
Riga digdigdig, riga digdig — far from home, far from home,
Riga digdigdig, riga digdig . . where's your dog, where's your dog?
Riga digdig —

VIRGINIA

(*hitting him with her blanket*) Oh Mr. Hagen, you old fool, sometimes I think you must be a re-tard, playing with toys and singsonging them looney-blooney jingle-dingles. (*She pulls out a tattered book from under the car seat.*) I prefer Miss Edna St. Vincent Millay.

ANNIVERSARY ON WEEDY HILL

SETH

Oh jeesus.

VIRGINIA

(*holding the book to her breast*) "What's this of death" —

SETH

(*in mock declamation*) "What's this of death" —

VIRGINIA

(*looks at him and he stops and chuckles*) "What's this of death" — (*faltering*) "What's this" — (*stops*) Knew it by heart once. (*finds the poem in the book*)
> "What's this of death, from you who never will die?
> Think you the wrist that fashioned you in clay,
> The thumb that set the hollow just that way
> In your full throat and lidded the long eye . ."*

(*Seth has pretended to fall asleep. Noticing this, Virginia leaps on him, covering his head with her blanket. Sound of freeway crash. Seth jumps away from Virginia, sending her sprawling.*)

SETH

Smashup, smashup on the freeway! (*grabbing his telescope and running to the edge of down right stage, looking out at the audience*)

VIRGINIA

(*picking herself up*) Bet I be safer out there than here. How many automobiles?

SETH

(*peering through the telescope*) Can't tell. But if you don't hear no ambulance pretty soon it can't be much of a smashup.

VIRGINIA

No bodies lying around, huh? You're getting too kill-crazy for me.

SETH

Well, them lousy cars pukin' up the air! People like me with asthma catchin' hell from them bastards. Good whiff of pure fresh air once in a while jus' for ol' time's sake'd be appreciated by one and all, you betcha. (*Virginia has a sudden thought and makes a feeble effort to clean up the place with a broom.*) Naw, nothin much, jes' tyin' up traffic a little. (*putting the telescope away*) Well, it's somethin' anyway. (*noticing Virginia's hopeless attempt at cleaning up*) What the hell you doin', Ginny?

VIRGINIA

I just remembered, Mr. Hagen. This is your anniversary.

SETH

Anniversary?

* From Sonnet XXXV by Edna St. Vincent Millay. *Collected Poems*, Harper & Row. Copyright 1923, 1951 by Edna St. Vincent Millay and Norma Millay Ellis.

73

VIRGINIA

Yes, the seventh. Seven years. That's how long you been living on this weedy hill.

SETH

Well, I'll be goddamned!

VIRGINIA

And some of the folks'll be dropping in to give you congratulations and all that. We have to neaten up the place a little.

SETH

Yeh sure, we don't want them rubby-dubs thinkin' I live in a dump.

VIRGINIA

Not many as lucky as you, Mr. Hagen.

SETH

Right. I gotta better view of the freeway than anybody else. Almost top of the hill. Low-cost high-rise. (*Virginia has another sudden thought. She stops sweeping and opens an old shoebox in which she keeps various mementos. She takes out something and faces Seth holding her hands behind her. He looks at her inquisitively. Gaily, like a child, she thrusts out both hands containing a big box of matches and a cigarette.*)

VIRGINIA

Happy Anniversary!

SETH

(*laughing*) Omigod! (*He tries to embrace her, but she shyly pulls away from him.*)

VIRGINIA

Now you got matches. (*begins sweeping again*)

SETH

What would I do without you, Ginny? If you'd throw away that damn poetry book, maybe I'd marry ya.

VIRGINIA

That would surely be the climax of my happy life.

SETH

Well, how long's it been since ya had a climax?

VIRGINIA

Shush up, you.

SETH

(*looking down at his crotch*) Shush up, Thunderclap! Hey, how about if I let the poor thing loose in the world, Virginia?

VIRGINIA

(*giggling and keeping away from him*) Don't you dare. I'm not as strong as I used to be. I might faint dead away. Haven't ever seen you without

74

them fine garments covering your shame. I have a suspicion there's nothing underneath.

SETH

Oh yes, there is, Ginny.

VIRGINIA

Just a bag-a-rag with a hairy old face on top.

SETH

There's something underneath all right. I can feel him squirming around in there every time he comes near you.

VIRGINIA

(*lashing out at him with her broom*) Go ahead then, bring him forth and I'll just exercise him a little with this.

SETH

(*retreating hastily*) Great cannonballs of white lightnin', woman . . look now, I ain't got no use for a pecker-whacker.

VIRGINIA

Well, just keep your doggy indoors when I'm around if you don't want him splintered.

SETH

(*laughing*) Yeh, guess yer right. Hardly worth gettin' outta my rented tuxedo and then back in jes' for 1-2-3, anyway. (*He reclines on the hammock, breathing a little heavily. He doesn't notice the change that has come over Virginia as she stands on the crest of the hill looking out at the sky and mumbling.*) Hoo boy, I'm whooshed out. Who'd think I once built my own beanery?

VIRGINIA

(*her mumbling becoming clear*) — how many were there? How many jumped on Virginia that night? How many? How — were there — how many —

SETH

Huh? Oh, Ginny, I'm sorry. Goddamn me, I didn't mean to stir ya up. I was only havin' fun with ya.

VIRGINIA

(*very agitated, turning and backing away*) They were all over her, on top of her, tearing and hitting — how many, how many, how many, how — (*screaming and crawling around on the ground*)

SETH

(*trying to catch her*) I don't know, Ginny — there was nobody around when I found ya. Now that was almost a year and a half ago — ya gotta put it outta yer head. (*She is huddled up on the car seat, sobbing and muttering. Seth is beside her, trying to get her attention.*) Ginny — Ginny? Ginny — (*Takes a stick of red licorice from his pocket and dangles it before her*

eyes. She quiets down and puts it in her mouth, sucking on it like a child.)
You know I'd never degrade you. (*pause*)

VIRGINIA

Yes. (*pause*) I know you wouldn't, Mr. Hagen.

SETH

There. That's better. (*claps his hands*) Now, how many's comin' to the party?

VIRGINIA

(*slowly*) Well, Minnie Skinny —

SETH

Minnie Skinny.

VIRGINIA

Yes. Said she'd come with her brother, the Leftover Eater —

SETH

Good, good.

VIRGINIA

And Cranberry Juice'll be here if he don't get lost like he always does. (*Seth laughs.*) But the Invisible Man can't make it.

SETH

How come not?

VIRGINIA

He's dead.

SETH

Oh.

VIRGINIA

They found him dead. Him and another piper.

SETH

The hell ya say. Jes' a kid.

VIRGINIA

They found him when somebody smelled something bad. He was dead three or four days, curled up tight under a bunch of weeds.

SETH

Phew. Yeh, now I remember, he was pretty low last few times he come here. Wouldn't eat, jes' guzzle that Bay Horse all the time. He drank the worst, gut-burnin' roachpiss anybody ever tasted. Well, he probably got down in a rut and couldn't get out. (*takes a pull from a half-pint whiskey bottle he finds under the car seat*) Probably didn't want to. (*offers Virginia the bottle*)

VIRGINIA

You better watch it, too. You've been hitting it pretty hard lately.

76

SETH

C'mon, I ain't no barrel-house stiff. I'm careful what I pour into me. Little red table wine spiked with a little somethin' else never hurt nobody. But I ain't no rubby-dub, Ginny, you know I ain't. That's why I'm so pretty.

VIRGINIA

(*dunking her licorice in the whiskey*) Blind Man Bluff and Lena the Lizard won't be coming, either.

SETH

How come not?

VIRGINIA

They went south.

SETH

Hit the rails?

VIRGINIA

Guess so. Said they couldn't take the smog no more.

SETH

Don't blame 'em. Where they gonna get away from it, though? Hey, how about Hershey Bar and Benny Butterfly — they comin'?

VIRGINIA

Haven't seen them around lately. Maybe they'll show up.

SETH

(*picking up a newspaper*) Shiii-et. Some anniversary party. Bet lotta the boys don't know about it even.

VIRGINIA

Oh — I'm sorry, Mr. Hagen.

SETH

Nah, that's all right — they'll get around to it. They always droppin' in to say hello and killin' a jug or two. Probably all pour in on me tomorrow or next day. (*Seth becomes absorbed in the newspaper and is at first unaware of Virginia staring at him. Finally he looks up.*) What the hell you starin' at?

VIRGINIA

Excuse me, Mr. Hagen. I was just wondering . .

SETH

Well, you're sure makin' a helluva racket doin' it. About what?

VIRGINIA

About all that money the man from the bank gave you.

SETH

Omigod, ya ain't goin' to start nittlin' me about that again, are ya? Nittle, nittle, nittle.

VIRGINIA

Why are you so secretive about it? You think I'm going to steal it from you?

SETH

(*gently*) I ain't got it, Ginny. How many times I gotta tell ya?

VIRGINIA

But I thought he said it was yours, that they'd been holding it for you for nearly ten years?

SETH

I rejected it. You read it in the sheets yerself. I give it back to the man. I told him to give it to the mission flophouse on San Pedro. I didn't want all that money interfering with our life here.

VIRGINIA

It would give you a chance to start all over again.

SETH

Sure it would — and go crazy all over again, too.

VIRGINIA

I don't want any of it if that's what you're thinking. I'm content just as I am. And you already done enough for me, finding me in that alley —

SETH

Aw hell, that did me more good than you —

VIRGINIA

I can't believe a grown man would refuse to take what belongs to him and make life easier for himself.

SETH

What life can be easier than this?

VIRGINIA

Oh, you know what I mean — a nice home —

SETH

Now please don't mention that. Don't talk about that life to me anymore. (*He takes a drink.*)

VIRGINIA

Stop teasing me, Mr. Hagen. You got the money, haven't you?

SETH

Dammit woman, I ain't — I ain't got it. I don't want it! I got all I need right here. Look, look here — (*produces a few coins from his pocket*) Here, see that — how much's there? A couple of quarters, dimes, pennies, about seventy-five cents. Right? But I'm rich. It's all the richer I want to be. (*throws the coins into the air and lies back in the hammock*) Enough for a short jug and a smoke.

ANNIVERSARY ON WEEDY HILL

VIRGINIA

But not enough for matches, huh? Mr. Hagen, I do believe you're berserk, really I do. (*She picks up the coins and puts them back in his hand. Then she sits on a high stack of newspapers that are tied together with cord and gently rocks the hammock Seth is lying in back and forth.*)

SETH

Virginia — you my friend, my valentine, the woman I share my plantation here with, who watches over me and —

VIRGINIA

You could take a bath more often.

SETH

Well, answer me — you that woman or not?

VIRGINIA

You know I am, Mr. Hagen.

SETH

Then please, I don't want to hear no more about that beanery, that "nice" life and all the rest of that crap. I made my choice and I'm glad of it. Sure, one of these days maybe I'll be dumb enough to wanta climb out of the bottom of the barrel, but right now, *no*, not right now. I'm not ready yet. Gotta rest up and have a drink for a few years more.

VIRGINIA

(*sighs and walks to the crest of the hill*) They ought to be coming pretty soon. (*Noticing Seth's pensive mood, she comes down to him again.*) Want a haircut, Mr. Hagen?

SETH

Naw, you cut too much around the ears.

VIRGINIA

Better get dressed then.

SETH

Leave me be, woman.

VIRGINIA

(*fooling with his hair*) Need a hedgerow cutter for that mess.

SETH

C'mon. Get my dicer, will ya, and never mind the insults. (*She picks up a battered hat from the chair.*) And my shroud, please. (*She picks up a shabby, torn coat and hands both items to him. Seth puts on the coat and hat.*) How's it look? (*She shrugs hopelessly.*) I dunno, I guess I'm still spooked, Gin. (*A rat scurries through the rubble.*)

VIRGINIA

Uh-huh — how is it that all your pets running around here don't spook you?

SETH

Oh, nothin' to fear there — I'm jes' another rat to them. (*Virginia goes behind the palm tree to change from her nightgown to a shapeless dress.*)

VIRGINIA

I still can't believe you give it away. (*Sound of voices offstage. Seth runs to the top of the hill.*)

MINNIE

(*offstage*) Ho-ho-ho up there.

SETH

Ho-ho-ho down there.

LEFTOVER EATER

(*offstage*) Hey, Cranberry, yer goin' the wrong way. The party's this way.

CRANBERRY JUICE

(*offstage*) M-m-my m-mouth or-rgan. I llost mmy m-mouth or-organ. (*Minnie Skinny enters. A prostitute, loud, profane, and full of fun. She jumps on Seth, wrapping her long legs around his waist.*)

MINNIE

Happy blueballed anniversary, you big-assed millionaire, you! (*licks his face*)

SETH

(*sputtering*) Hey — hey, yer ruinin' my complexion.

MINNIE

(*getting off Seth*) Okay, up yours, I'll love up Ginny. (*jumps on the car seat and grabs Virginia*) C'mon, sweetie, let's me and you go off into the bushes. To hell with the crappy party.

VIRGINIA

Oh, get away from me, Minnie Skinny.

MINNIE

(*clinging to her*) Just you and me, baby doll. You show me yours and I'll show you mine.

VIRGINIA

(*extricating herself and moving away with her shoebox of ribbons*) Business must be bad for you, you got all that energy.

MINNIE

I guess I better give up on people. Ya got any dogs or goats around here wanna get laid? Jeez, a gal's gotta get a good poke now and then for memory's sake if nothin' else. (*Enter Leftover Eater followed by Cranberry Juice. They both carry two bottles.*)

EATER

Seth ol' buddy!

SETH

Here they are — the kids from Main Street!

ANNIVERSARY ON WEEDY HILL

EATER

(*holding two bottles aloft*) Here's my donation and this one's Minnie's. (*He comes down off the hill but is stopped and pushed back by Seth.*)

SETH

Get back there, Leftover Eater!

EATER

Hey, what's bitin' you?

SETH

Get up there and wipe your feet before you come in the house.

EATER

House? Oh yeh — sure — I forgot. (*turns to Cranberry*) Wipe, you bum. (*They shuffle their feet on the ground.*) How about my dumb sister there. I bet she didn't wipe —

MINNIE

(*airily*) Ladies don't walk in dogshit.

SETH

(*laughing*) Yer sis don't have dirty feet, jes' a dirty mouth and she already wiped that off on my face.

MINNIE

(*throwing herself on Seth again*) Hey, pretty good for a wedge!

CRANBERRY

(*a smiling, stuttering mentally retarded little man; one leg is wrapped in old rags*) I d-didn't ffferget, ddid I? See — sssee — I al-wways wwipe my fffeet, don't I ddddon't I, S-Seth?

SETH

Sure do, Cranberry Juice.

EATER

(*lanky, gaunt, sarcastic*) Find yer harmonica?

CRANBERRY

(*wiping alongside Eater*) Huh? N-no — was lllookin' f-for mmy m-mouth orrr-gan. It w-was in mmy pocket all the t-time. Llook, Seth, I ffound two jjjugs. (*holds up his two bottles*)

SETH

(*getting Minnie off him*) Great.

MINNIE

In a pig's ass he found them. The creep stole them from Honey Dew after somebody coldcocked Honey and left him for dead behind the burleeque house.

CRANNIE

H-h-how'd ya k-know that?

MINNIE

You told me, condom head.

CRANNIE

(*laughing delightedly*) Oh yyeh, I re-mmmember.

SETH

Okay, ya wiped enough. C'mon in and put yer bombs over here on the bar.

EATER

(*throwing his arms around Seth*) Seth, you rich son of a bitch!

SETH

Christ, you chickens are flyin' already!

MINNIE

Well, honey, when we go socializin' on Moneybags Seth and his Miss Virginia No-Screw, we need a little advanced shootoff to meet all the famous Hollywood stars at the big fart-out, don't you think now? (*pulls Seth down on the couch*) C'mon, bite the pretty titty, baby!

SETH

HELP! (*Virginia pulls Minnie off Seth. The two women glare at each other for a moment and then move apart.*)

EATER

(*having deposited his bottles on the "bar," he bangs two cans together*) Who wants what? We got —

SETH

Wait a minute, wait a minute. Who in hell elected you bartender?

EATER

Oh yeh, I forgot, we gotta match for it.

CRANNIE

(*after putting his bottles on the bar*) I dddidn't forget, I ddd-ddidn't forget. We mmatch fffor it, ddon't we S-Seth, ddon't wwe? I dddidn't ffforget. (*Eater glares at him.*)

EATER

I'll keep fergittin' and you keep rememberin' and sooner or later I'll twist yer fuggin' ears off. (*Crannie blows a teasing note on his harmonica and Eater throws a kick at him.*)

SETH

All right, that's enough bore-assin'. How we goin' to match this time?

EATER

Like always — spittin' over the hill.

SETH

Naw — somebody always gets it in the eye.

ANNIVERSARY ON WEEDY HILL

MINNIE

How about pissin' in a tin can?

SETH

Hey, not bad, Min.

VIRGINIA

Oh peewh. (*noticing Crannie placing a can on a rock and working at his fly*) Not in the house! It'll bring all the flies in!

SETH

(*grabbing the can off the rock and tapping Crannie lightly in the crotch — all in one motion*) Don't fret, Ginny, we'll have the Olympics on the other side of the hill. C'mon, gang, Virginia works hard keepin' the house in shape, so let's go. (*They head for the top of the hill.*) Allrightee, I'll mark off a couple of feet. (*He paces off and disappears offstage.*) One gets closest is bartender. (*returns*) You first, Crannie. (*Crannie goes to the edge of the hill, just barely visible, with his back to the audience. The other two men stand alongside of him.*)

MINNIE

While the meatheads are drainin' their hoses, let's me and you get the party goin', Ginny.

EATER

C'mon, peanut, before it gets too dark to see the can.

MINNIE

What'd ya like, Ginny?

SETH

Ya got it out yet?

CRANNIE

S-sure hhave. (*He turns to Eater who jumps back.*)

EATER

Don't point it at me, goddamn it! D'ya see that, Seth?

SETH

Yeh, Cran boy, you got that fearsome thing registered?

VIRGINIA

(*drinking*) Sweet vermouth.

EATER

Uncork it, for crissakes. (*He and Seth try to take Crannie's pants off.*)

CRANNIE

(*wriggling*) Y-ya makin' me llllaugh . . quit it . . I ccccan't pp-ppee wh-when I'm lllaughin' —

SETH

Wait a minute, let's go back to the Department of Water and Power and refuel. (*They cross back to the bar.*) Excuse us, ladies, we gotta reload.

83

VIRGINIA

Come on, Minnie, get away from those animals.

MINNIE

Can't I watch? Ya gotta have a referee, don't ya?

SETH

No thanks, Min, you'd cheat for yer brother.

MINNIE

No I won't.

EATER

Whatta ya mean ya *won't*?

SETH

(*after they drink*) Okay men, now bounce around a little. Gotta put a head on. (*They jump up and down.*) Now a few smacks on the old bladder. (*slap their sides*) Okay, back up to the startin' line! (*As they head back to their positions, Virginia picks up her broom and attacks them.*)

VIRGINIA

Get away from here! You're not giving *me* a thrill peeing all over the place!

SETH

(*as they run offstage hooting and yelling*) All right then, we'll have to fire uphill —

EATER

That ain't gonna be easy . .

VIRGINIA

Crazy loons. (*Offstage ad libs are heard.*)

MINNIE

Boys gotta be boys, Virginia. Which is jake with me. And I like girls, too, y'know. (*She pinches one of Virginia's breasts.*)

VIRGINIA

(*slapping her hand away*) Ow! Behave yourself! (*sits on the ground behind the car seat, sipping from a bottle of vermouth*)

SETH

(*offstage*) Ready, Crannie? On yer mark — GO!

CRANNIE

(*offstage*) Th-that's ttttoo fffast!

EATER

(*offstage*) Christ, give him a count.

SETH

(*offstage*) Minnie'll do the trick. (*reappears onstage*) Hey, Min, be a good kid and give the lad a slow count, will ya?

MINNIE

(*crossing to the top of the hill*) Sure, Seth. My big chance and I ain't gonna

muff it. Here it comes, Crannie. (*Seth runs offstage again.*) Ya braced?
(*doing a slow, exaggerated grind*) One-nnnnnnnnn — Two-ooooo —
THA-REEEEEEEEEEEEEEEEEEE!

EATER

(*offstage*) Whatta shot! (*Minnie jumps back.*)

MINNIE

Man the lifeboats!

SETH

(*reappearing and measuring back by foot*) Ya overshot, Crannie, but ya
had a helluva arc on it. (*He exits again.*)

MINNIE

C'mon, Eater, show 'em what a real cannon can do.

EATER

(*offstage; an empty milk container flies onstage*) You ain't needed no more!

MINNIE

(*laughing and rejoining Virginia*) Hey, Gin, has Seth figgered out yet what
we're gonna do with it?

VIRGINIA

What? What are you talking about?

SETH

(*offstage*) Let fly, Eater, soon's yer lined up.

MINNIE

C'mon — that money the man give him. He showed it to ya, didn't he?

VIRGINIA

No, I haven't seen it. Says he didn't want to take it.

SETH

(*offstage*) Good shot — ya kicked up a lotta dust. My turn now.

MINNIE

Oh hell, don't be so dumb — sure he's sayin' that. Think he wants every
rummy-stiff on the stem to know he's got it?

VIRGINIA

But he says he gave it to a flophouse.

MINNIE

That's jes' a blind — wake up, for crissakes.

SETH

(*offstage*) Bull's-eye!

CRANNIE

(*offstage*) Yyou wwwin, S-Seth. And up-h-hill, tttoo.

VIRGINIA

Why would he hide it from me?

MINNIE

Maybe becuz ya talk too much and in no time the old meatball'd be fightin' off a hundred jackrollers roarin' in from Main Street — that's why he ain't showed it to ya, I bet.

VIRGINIA

I find that hard to believe.

EATER

(*offstage*) You been practicin'.

SETH

(*as they reenter*) Hell I have. First time I laid eyes on that can. Okay, I'm bartender and the first round's on the house.

EATER

Ladies, meet the winner and still champeen, Wet-Pants Hagen!

SETH

Now ya know the rules when I'm tendin' bar. No swearin' plus anythin' else ya might think of. I run a nice clean place. (*Minnie guffaws.*) All right, whatta we got here? (*sniffs at the bottle Crannie has been holding*) Goddamn it, Crannie, you still drinking gasoline?

CRANNIE

I s-swipe it fffrom — fffrom —

SETH

Yer gonna go blind one of these days. Yer gonna blow yer nose and yer eyeballs'll plop right into yer lap and yer pecker'll shrivel up and turn to sawdust — but not in my bar, nosirreee. (*throws Crannie's bottle offstage*)

CRANNIE

Aw, what'd ya — wwwwwhat'd ya —

SETH

(*pulling Crannie back as he goes for bottle*) Never mind, we got plenty good stuff here. (*drapes a rag over his arm and imitates a waiter*) I'm takin' orders. Minnie?

MINNIE

(*the grand lady*) Oh, I'll have a pink screwdriver, *boy*.

SETH

One pink screwdriver. And the little lady here?

VIRGINIA

(*not quite with it*) Just anything. I kind of like that sweet vermouth.

EATER

What the hell kind of a drink is that?

SETH

Yeh, the horseface gentleman is right. How about — let's see — a Hong Kong Swizzle Dong?

ANNIVERSARY ON WEEDY HILL

VIRGINIA

(*joining the fun*) With crushed ice, Mr. Bartender.

SETH

With my bare hands. Eater, you want a Kangaroo Blast on the rocks, right?

EATER

Yeh, with a twist of lime.

SETH

Needless to say. Crannie, you and me'll have the specials of the house, a Minnehaha Maiden's Blush and a Honolulu Hoolulu Jackass.

CRANNIE

Oh b-boy!

SETH

(*motioning to Eater*) Okay, Eater, let's get to work. (*Seth discards his hat and coat and gets a bottle from the sewing machine. Eater gets an old sink lying on the ground far down left stage and puts it on the tree stump as Seth empties his bottle into it. Minnie pokes holes into a can of mix and pours it into the sink. Crannie and Virginia bring a box from down right and put it between the car seat and the sink, and spread papers on it. Virginia places a pan of vegetables from Seth's garden on the box. Eater has been bringing bottles from the sewing machine for Seth to pour into the sink. The liquid should be in various colors. The activity has a certain efficient gravity to it. Eater discovers a large water jug offstage containing a small amount of water. He carries it to the sink and carefully pours a drop into the brew. He is rewarded with a shout of approval from the others and he puts the jug back in place. Crannie plays on his harmonica. Eater tosses Seth a plumber's helper to stir the concoction with and Seth throws it right back at him. Ginny hands a battered ladle to Seth which he uses as a stirrer. Eater brings over an armful of cans to Seth who pours the brew and hands out the cans.*) Fill up and pray. Here's yer screwdriver, Minnie.

MINNIE

(*sniffing at her drink*) Umm. Smells real delicate.

SETH

Thank you, Min, I pride myself.

EATER

(*as Minnie starts to drink*) Hey, wait for the toast, will ya?

MINNIE

Oh yeh. (*Raising her can*) Up yers. (*Eater draws back his hand as if to hit her.*) Watch it.

SETH

Virginia — what'd you order now — uh — Hong Kong —?

VIRGINIA
Swizzle Swizzle.

SETH
There you are.

VIRGINIA
Many thanks.

SETH
My pleasure. Now — Eater, there's yer slop. Cranberry. And me. Oh, wait a minute — (*Looks around on the ground and finds a used lemon. He plops it into Eater's can*) Twist it yerself.

EATER
(*ruefully*) Thanks.

SETH
Okay now, let's settle down to a little quiet boozing.

EATER
(*raising his can*) Here's to Seth, King of the Beaneries! The richest bum in the world! Here's to Seth on Weedy Hill — how many years?

VIRGINIA
Seven. To the finest gentleman, the kindest —

SETH
Yeh, yeh, pipe down and drink. (*All except Virginia bolt their drinks.*)

EATER
(*gasping*) Jeesus!

MINNIE
Oh burn, burn, dig in, baby, oooh, oooooooh!

SETH
(*falling over*) I'm dead.

CRANNIE
(*blithely refilling his can*) G-good sstuff, ggggood s-stuff. You mmake g-good sstuff, S-Seth.

VIRGINIA
(*sipping*) That's what you all get for gulping. Just sip it. Blow and sip. That way you taste the flavor.

EATER
Screw the flavor. I wan' another kick in the nuts. (*drinks; same results*) Jeesus! Few more jolts and I'll sleep like I was never born tonight. (*Minnie suddenly erupts into a stripper's bumps and grinds dance.*)

CRANNIE
L-look at ol' Minnie dance. L-look at ol' Mmmin. B-boy, she's gggood.

EATER
(*looking up*) She's rotten. (*After gyrating clear around the area, Minnie*

wiggles her rump dangerously over the sink and almost falls into it. Eater yanks her away just in time.) Keep outta the booze, goddamn it! Who the hell wants to drink that muck with yer ass floatin' around in it? This is our rich buddy's best anniversary, so try to act like you was almost human. Stay the hell outta the booze, y'hear? (*Minnie gives him a bronx cheer. There's a menacing pause as Eater stares at her.*) I think maybe ya already had enough. Sleep by yerself tonight. I don't wanna hear yer fuckin' screams.

CRANNIE

(*getting another drink*) Y-yeh, yyou'll gget — gget — ggggget — n-n-n —

SETH

Nightmares?

CRANNIE

Y-yeh, yyyou k-know all ttthe w-words, S-Seth.

SETH

Sure know all about them, all right.

EATER

Had some creepers?

SETH

You betcha. Get a whopper almost every night. (*Minnie guffaws.*) No no, I'm talkin' about nightmares. Like last night I dreamt I woke up early in the mornin' and I hear somebody callin' and I stand up and my pants fall off. I start walkin' and turn around and see my pants with my legs in 'em walkin' off in the other direction —

EATER

Christ, I'm glad I didn't run into either one of ya.

MINNIE

I always get the same dream about a train —

EATER

I'm listenin' to *his* dream now, y'mind?

MINNIE

(*ignoring him*) — 'n I can see the motorman's face — jes' the face which looks like Pa — and the train's goin' backwards away from me —

CRANNIE

Choo-choo-choo, choo, choo, choo — (*Eater throws a pebble at him.*)

SETH

— then all of a sudden there's a big black hole in the middle of my chest and I'm stuffin' rags, papers, bottles, cans — anythin' — into it — (*Virginia moves restlessly across the crest of the hill, her figure silhouetted against the changing hue of the sky.*) — but it keeps gettin' bigger until there's nothing else — I turn into a big black hole — jes' a hole stumblin' around —

89

EATER

Jeez —

MINNIE

— it starts movin' slow at first 'n I know I can make it easy —

CRANNIE

(*under his breath*) — choo-choo-choo —

SETH

Then like a flash everything's gone and I'm on the bottom of the ocean — (*Crannie dozes off. Minnie is absorbed in her own dream. Virginia wanders around, humming tunelessly to herself. Eater tries to focus on Seth's dream.*) — and it's quiet like an underwater graveyard 'n a dead fish, a marlin or somethin', floats by and I poke my finger into his eye — .

VIRGINIA

(*stops singing*) David was pale and thin —

EATER

Who?

SETH

— 'n then I'm a little kid again sleepin' in my room —

EATER

'S all happened last night?

MINNIE

—'n Pa keeps lookin' at me 'n the train keeps movin' away —

EATER

(*giving it up*) Oh shit.

SETH

— 'n I hear the floor creakin' like somebody movin' around in the room and I'm scared — (*his voice now an intense whisper*) and all of a sudden I see somebody comin' at me 'n it's my old buddy, Jerry Angelus, we was in the war together, 'n he holds his hands out to me but his fingers turn into long rusty nails with blood pourin' outta them 'n he stabs at me 'n I'm screamin' — screamin' and runnin' my scared ass outta the room yellin' momma, momma, momma!!! (*Seth blindly beats on Crannie's bandaged foot.*)

CRANNIE

(*waking up and leaping away*) Ow — ow — S-Seth — my f-f-foot — yer hurtin' —

SETH

(*coming out of it*) Hey — jeez — I'm sorry, Crannie — I didn't mean — what the hell was I — my god!

EATER

(*disgusted*) Dumb fart — put his foot in the fire last week —

SETH

Why don't ya put some clean rags on it? (*Virginia comes over to look at Crannie's foot.*)

CRANNIE

Oh, it's g-gettin' bbbetter —

EATER

Yeh — well, y'won't feel anythin' after they hack it off. (*There's a long pause as the group resumes drinking.*) Uh — which war was you in, Seth?

SETH

The big one.

EATER

(*a beat*) Well — which the hell one was that?

SETH

Two. The big blast. Eighty-Fifth Infantry. Custer Division. Shoulder patch was CD — 'n I don't mean Civil Defense. In sunny Italy — from the toe to the top of the boot — drank it bone dry — god, god, god — (*Minnie is looking at the toy soldier.*)

MINNIE

Y'play with dolls, Seth?

SETH

(*laughing*) Give'm a twist and put'm on the ground, Min. (*She does this and the toy marches.*)

    Rigadigdig, rigadigdig, soldier boy, soldier boy,
    Rigadigdig, rigadigdig, where's yer dog, where's yer dog?
    Rigadigdig, rigadigdig —

(*On a dark impulse, Crannie suddenly kicks over the toy and stomps on it.*)

MINNIE

Hey — ! (*Crannie backs away as Seth stares at him. Then Seth covers the toy with a newspaper.*)

SETH

— dig a hole, dig a hole —

MINNIE

(*attempting to revive the party's spirit, she refills her can*) Here's to seven years on Weedy Hill.

EATER

(*holding up his can*) Yeh!

CRANNIE

I ww-wan-na be inna w-war, t-too. W-wan-na be a mmmmachy-

91

gun-nnner — mmmmmachy-gunnnn — (*He makes a noise of a machine gun.*) Ratttatatatatatatatat —

EATER

Oh, here comes the horseshit again. (*Crannie goes berserk with his simulated machine gun. Eater slaps him in the face.*) C'MON, C'MON, C'MON!! (*Crannie snaps out of it.*) Boy, they're gonna put you away one of these days. Machygunner. Ya gotta have at least a *corner* of a brain before they — before they — you, hell — you got oatmeal over yer nose. (*Crannie grins up at him.*) Rattattat my ass. (*Eater turns away from him.*) I need a smoke. Anybody got a snipe?

SETH

Yeh. (*Seth takes a cigarette out of his pocket and breaks it in half. Hands one half to Eater. They put the butts in their mouths and stand staring at each other for a moment. Then Eater makes a flicking motion with his thumb and forefinger.*) Oh yeh, a glim. (*Seth gets the box of safety matches Virginia gave him. The two men light up. Seth coughs.*) Damn bronchitis.

EATER

How's it feel to be handed a pile of dough, buddy?

SETH

What?

EATER

Some anniversary present, huh?

SETH

You talkin' about — (*A rat crosses Minnie's path.*)

MINNIE

(*leaping up on the car seat*) OH JEESUS, CAN'T YA DO SOMETHIN' ABOUT THEM THINGS, SETH?

SETH

(*turning to her*) What things?

MINNIE

What things? Ya mean ya didn't see them? Didn't nobody see 'em? They jes' galloped through here like a herd of wild-assed bulldogs. (*clutching herself*) Christ, I dunno. This booze ain't doin' nothin' for me.

SETH

Pay no heed, Min. When they look like green jackrabbits then ya got trouble.

EATER

(*suddenly alert*) Hey look! There's a slinky bastard right over there.

CRANNIE

W-where, wwwhere?

EATER

Over there. Look at him starin' at me.

ANNIVERSARY ON WEEDY HILL

CRANNIE

Ooh y-yeh, I sssee h-him.

EATER

(*snarling and crawling toward a clump of newspapers*) Look at those glinty little eyes . . ugly mother-grabbin' cockeyed little son of a bitch . . (*He lunges at the papers and thrashes around.*) I got him! I got him!

MINNIE

(*she and Virginia almost run into each other*) YA GOT HIM? WHAT THE HELL YA GONNA DO WITH HIM?

EATER

(*coming up with nothing, the papers floating to the ground*) Shit, he got away . . could feel his spongy little belly right in my hands — (*shows Virginia, who shudderingly turns away*) right there —

CRANNIE

It w-was sssstarin' all-rrright —

SETH

Yeh — stare ya right outta yer skullcap —

EATER

Creepy bastards —

SETH

There's a dead one on the other side of the hill — eyes bugged out — hair frizzled and standin' on end — body stiff as a stone, petrified —

EATER

(*looking around*) Where the hell did he go?

SETH

— I threw him against a tree and he cracked up in three parts like chinaware — y'know if one of them gives off a bad smell other rats stand around and stare at him — they jes' kinda pile hate-stares into him until he dries up dead. (*chuckles to himself*) Yep — jes' plain, ordinary folk like the rest of us, them buggers — they ain't bothered me and Ginny, yet — guess we been accepted — (*Seth lies down beside Virginia who is sitting in the legless chair next to the sewing machine, and rests his head in her lap. The sky turns rosier. A late afternoon hush settles on the group. Eater stands stupified behind the car seat. Crannie plays softly on his harmonica while he sits beside the tree stump. Minnie lies in the hammock watching Eater under lidded eyes.*)

EATER

(*moving aimlessly around the area*) Rigadigdig — rigaliglag — sojerboy, sojerboy, dig hole — dig hole — dig yer dog — (*Spots a crumpled paper bag. Picks it up and slowly unravels it, looks into it, and then lets it fall to the ground again. He heads for a seat but Minnie sticks her foot out and prevents him from sitting. She motions to the dozing Seth. Eater crosses to Seth and slaps him on the behind.*) Hey Seth, Seth ol' boy — hey, wake, y'old Weedyfart! (*Seth looks up at him.*) Yer the greatest — y'know that? Yer the greatest. (*Seth smilingly puts his head back on Virginia's lap.*) Lissen — when ya — when ya gonna — tell us — about — (*Getting no response from Seth, Eater turns helplessly to Minnie. Then he sees Crannie and gets an idea.*) Hey, Crannie, c'mon, show what ya learned last week. Hey, hey, Seth, look at this. (*He motions Crannie to get up.*)

CRANNIE

W-what I lllearned?

EATER

Yeh, you know, like a traffic cop.

CRANNIE

Oh-oh yyeh, yyeh — (*Crannie gets up and does an elaborate, though uncoordinated, imitation of an officer directing traffic. He uses his harmonica as a whistle and gyrates his arms wildly moving and stopping "traffic."*)

EATER

Haw! I caught him doin' that last week on Sixth and Main. He was standin' on the corner watchin' the cop and doin' everythin' he was. People was laughin' and tellin' him to go into the street to help the cop — and that's jes' what the woodhead starts to do. I yanked him away before the cop kills him. Look at him.

SETH

(*laughing and clapping his hands*) 'Atta boy, Crannie, he knows the score — everything's a game, ain't it, Cran baby?

CRANNIE

(*getting more frantic and laughing hysterically*) Y-yeh, yyyeh, s-sure is, s-sure is —

EATER

(*his mood changing abruptly — angered by Seth's flattery of Crannie*) You stink, you little mutt. Yer the dirtiest lookin' skunk I ever — yer disgustin' — I shouldn't be seen with ya — (*Grinning, Crannie motions him to move on with the traffic. Eater grabs him by the shirt.*) Y'know somethin'? I think yer flippin'.

CRANNIE

Fflip-pin'?

EATER

Yeh, flippin'.

CRANNIE

(*still grinning*) H-How'ddddya ffig-gger? (*pause*)

94

ANNIVERSARY ON WEEDY HILL

EATER

How do I figger yer flippin'?

CRANNIE

Yyyeh, how d-dya ffig-gger? (*pause*)

EATER

Yer always grinnin'.

CRANNIE

G-grin-nin'?

EATER

Yeh. Ya grin at everythin'. (*pause*) Couple of days ago I saw ya grinnin' at a garbage can.

CRANNIE

A gg-garbage cccan?

EATER

Yeh. (*pause*) Anybody that grins at garbage cans — (*pause*) I figger's gotta be flippin'. (*Crannie's grin fades away and he slowly turns away from eater. Pause.*)

VIRGINIA

(*crossing to Crannie and patting him on the head*) David was thin but he never cried —

MINNIE

(*emerging from her own lethargy*) Why am I always missin' the train?

EATER

(*stretching out on the hammock*) What?

MINNIE

I gotta make this train. I got all my bags and boxes and I gotta make this train. But I always miss it.

VIRGINIA

(*moving about*) I loved my first pair of high heels —

EATER

A bunch o' nuts in this dump.

MINNIE

At home I'm runnin' away after stickin' Pa in the leg — but in this dream, this goddamn dream, I keep missin' the train — but I didn't really miss it — I made it, I made it and got away from Pa — but in the *dream* I miss it.

CRANNIE

Choo-choo-choo —

MINNIE

And I run my ass off. Train pulls away. I chase it. My legs get heavy and I fall into holes — and I always miss the same cottonpickin' train. (*pause*) Anybody figger that one out?

EATER

Whyncha grab the next train?

MINNIE

(*turning on him balefully*) Whyncha grab yerself and take another shot at that tin can?

EATER

Huh?

MINNIE

You sure yer my brother? Oh boy — look, it's a dream — a wart-titted nightmare — how can I — oh — you — you — BLAECH! (*Eater stares at her and then slaps her, knocking her to the ground. Nobody gets excited about it.*)

SETH

(*taking a drink*) Nice to see you two gettin' along so good.

VIRGINIA

I don't dream anymore.

EATER

Good. Another dream and I puke.

VIRGINIA

But I remember a lot of things.

EATER

Jeesus —

VIRGINIA

My Auntie Louise gave me my first pair of high heels. Snow-white and so elegant — (*becoming fragmented in her story*) And David was small but he — "What's this of death, from you who never will die? Think you — uh — think — " (*She stops and looks for her book.*)

MINNIE

(*jumping up*) Here's to Weedy Seth's seven hills on — w'hell am I sayin'? To seven Seth's seedy weedy — oh, fergit it. Boy, some party. C'mon, let's have a little noise before Ginny finds that crappy poem. C'mon, Eater, wake up, for crissakes. Hey, everybody, dya meet my big brother, the Leftover Eater? He's got a real name someplace, but who the hell cares about that? Eater, ya low-hung son of a bitch, ya hit me, now dance with me. (*pulls him out of the hammock*)

EATER

(*pushing her away*) Shove off.

MINNIE

Aw, ball me, Eater. Somebody's gotta do it, I'm starvin' to death. I wanna

96

be loved, I wanna be pumped, wumped, and jabooed. Please, Eater. (*She backs him against the ladder that leans against the billboard.*)

EATER

(*pushing her away again*) Not here, ya creepy haybag, yer right out in the open, what the hell's matter with ya — ain't ya shamed of nothin'?

MINNIE

Shamed? Ya owe me, don't ya? I stuck a knife in Pa's leg when he was beatin' yer ass off fer jumpin' me on Ma's bedspread, didn't I? 'Member that?

CRANNIE

(*refilling at the sink*) Y-yeh, and dya 'mmmemmber about the tttime ya mmmade yer mma gg-go dddown on ya, tt-tell about ttthat, Eater —

EATER

(*stares at him for a second and then charges*) I'll kill ya!

SETH

(*jumping between them*) Hey, lay off, you guys.

CRANNIE

(*his drink flying out of his hands*) Hhhe told mme all aaabout it — wh-what's he ssore fffor?

EATER

I didn't do nothin' like that, Seth.

CRANNIE

Y-ya tttol' me ya d-ddid. Ya tol' me yyer m-mma ggot ddown and —

EATER

Ya stinkin' mission-stiff pervert! (*He gets away from Seth, knocks Crannie to the ground, and falls on top of him.*)

SETH

HEY HEY HEY! (*Everybody joins in the brawl, trying to keep Eater from killing Crannie.*)

VIRGINIA

Don't fight, boys, we're all friends —

CRANNIE

(*pumping his arms furiously*) I ain't nnno mmmmis-sion-ssstiff — I'mm a mmachy-g-gunn —

EATER

(*shoving him onto the car seat*) Yer a half-wit mission-stiff 'n ya always was — (*Seth keeps Eater away from Crannie while Virginia runs around in circles at the top of the hill. Minnie, sexually aroused by the fight, jumps on Crannie on the car seat.*)

MINNIE

C'mon now, Crannie, c'mon, baby, hang onto yerself, I love ya, sweetie, hmm, hmm —

CRANNIE

(*coming up for air*) D-did *you* kkknow hhhe mm-made yer mmmma gggo —

EATER

(*falls on top of Minnie and reaches over to grab Crannie's head*) Ya fleadung, I'll pull yer tongue outta yer fuckin' head —

SETH

(*astride Eater, trying to pull him off*) No more parties for you, goddamn you, Eater! (*Eater has his hand in Crannie's mouth, trying to get at his tongue.*)

CRANNIE

Oog wuh gah — (*Seth is hitting Eater in the arm. Minnie heaves upward and manages to extricate herself from the pileup.*)

MINNIE

I DIDN'T ASK FOR A GANG-BANG, YOU BASTARDS! (*limping away, hands on her back*) Christ, somethin's broke. (*Seth finally tears Eater away from Crannie and sends him sprawling up center stage where he falls against Virginia. They both crash to the ground. Virginia leaps away from him, screaming and scrambling down right toward the ladder.*)

VIRGINIA

DON'T TOUCH ME! I CAN'T STAND IT. KEEP AWAY FROM ME! (*Seth runs to her, but she holds him at bay.*) I'll scratch your eyes out. Y'hear? Don't touch me!

SETH

Ginny, Ginny!

VIRGINIA

(*running up the ladder*) Don't anybody touch me! My mommy's got a gun! Somebody touched me, somebody touched me — (*She breaks down into sobs.*)

SETH

(*after letting her cry herself out*) Okay, Ginny, okay now, nobody's gonna touch you, nobody's gonna lay a finger on ya, not while I'm around, I promise ya. (*The others have been shocked into silence by Virginia's outburst. Crannie crawls off the car seat and moves toward Virginia and Seth.*)

CRANNIE

W-want mme to ppplay ss-ssome-ththin' qquiet, Ggg-ginny?

SETH

(*leading Virginia off the ladder and to the hammock*) No, jes' get the hell

away, she'll be okay. C'mon, Ginny, easy does it, ain't nobody gonna
worry ya. Now now, quiet down —

MINNIE

(*the three get drinks and retreat to the far side of the stage*) "Don't touch
me, don't touch me." Jeesus — somebody must've rammed her good. How
come nothin' like that happens to me?

EATER

Shaddup.

MINNIE

Well, anyway, we give the party a shot in the ass, didn't we?

VIRGINIA

I'm sorry, Mr. Hagen, you know how I am about —

SETH

I know, I know —

VIRGINIA

I'm so ashamed.

SETH

Nothin' to be shamed about. Here, take a sip. (*Hands her a can. She drinks
slowly.*)

MINNIE

When ya goin' to ask him?

EATER

Who the hell's had a chance? I thought *he'd* say somethin' by now.

VIRGINIA

Mr. Eater there — he's got a mean streak. I do believe he's a mean man.

SETH

Naw, he ain't really . .

VIRGINIA

Look at the way he treats Mr. Juice . .

SETH

Aah, that's jes' his way of takin' care of him. A mean mouth don't always
make a mean man, Gin —

MINNIE

(*to Eater*) C'mon, start things rollin'. Spill the plan to him.

EATER

Yeh, yeh — the plan — (*looks at Minnie*) Jeez, do somethin' with yer face,
will ya? (*Hurt, Minnie takes a cracked little compact from her pocket and
inspects her face.*)

EATER

(*muttering*) The plan, the plan —

99

SETH

Feelin' better?

VIRGINIA

Yes. You're a gentleman, Mr. Hagen.

SETH

That's because there's a lady in the neighborhood.

VIRGINIA

(*after a beat*) I think it's time I go away.

SETH

(*startled*) What? The hell you say!

VIRGINIA

You don't need me.

SETH

Hell I don't. I'd burn my guts out with Crannie's gasoline if you wasn't here — never eat nothin' — fall down — and all anybody'd find'd be some splinty sticks of bones and maggoty hair under an old hat 'n coat — if you was to leave me.

VIRGINIA

(*thinks about it for a second*) Well — then I'll stay.

MINNIE

C'mon will ya, I'm runnin' down —

EATER

How dya think I feel? Can't even — wait a minute — let me catch my breath — (*lurches to his feet*) Okay, let's go — friendly — nice and friendly —

SETH

(*as the three approach*) Oh oh, here comes the Board of Directors —

EATER

(*under his breath to Minnie*) Give another toast or somethin' . .

MINNIE

Here's to — uh — uh — here's to — uh — uh —

SETH

I'll drink to that.

CRANNIE

(*singing*) Hap-py Bbbirth-dday to Sseth. Hap-ppy Birth-ddday —

MINNIE

Anniversary, anniversary, not his birthday —

EATER

(*giving Crannie the elbow*) Jeesus!

CRANNIE

Oh — yyyeh — (*They all sing the song, including Virginia lying in the hammock.*)

EATER

(*as they embrace Seth*) Yer the buddy, Seth, ol' buddy. How many years we know ya, huh? (*Virginia keeps on singing after the others have stopped.*)

SETH

Well — let's see —

EATER

That's right — plenty, right? Plenty. We all knowed Buddy Seth plenty years, right, gang?

MINNIE

I feel like I know Buddy Seth all my life.

CRANNIE

Bud-ddy's my bbbest b-budddy —

EATER

Everybody's best buddy. The salt of the earth — if it wasn't for ol' —

SETH

I guess we're all good buddies, huh?

EATER

Betcha. You always been our boy, buddy boy. Now look, we been thinkin' about that luck that come upon ya — (*Eater walks Seth, arm in arm, up and down the stage with Minnie and Crannie stumbling along behind.*)

SETH

(*laughing as Eater, arm in arm, walks him around some more*) Couldn't be you got an idea or two?

MINNIE

(*not really hearing Seth*) No no, Seth baby, listen to Eater . . once every hundred years the baboon comes up with an idea —

EATER

This ain't jes' for me, Seth, it's for all of us — especially for you, becuz you don't have to do nuttin' —

SETH

Jes' hand it over, right?

EATER

No no — bud-*dy*!

SETH

(*knowingly*) Bud-*dy*.

EATER

— agreement — investment — yer gonna double yer sock —

SETH

Which I ain't got —

MINNIE

The hell ya ain't — it was in the sheets and we saw it —

SETH

And didn't ya see where I give it to the mission on San Pedro?

MINNIE

That's baloney.

SETH

(*roaring with laughter*) Everybody believes what they wanna believe . . I even got some letters . . goddamn mailman near broke his hump trying to get up this mountain. One letter asks me if I remember when I was a boy and why don't I give him the cush to fix up a boys' club. The guy says they'll let me live in the back if I keep it clean. Ain't that sweet?

EATER

Wotta creep! "Remember when you was a boy!"

SETH

And some gal wants to name her baby after me if I'll send her some pitch to marry the guy that knocked her up.

MINNIE

C'mon — yer kiddin'.

SETH

I guess nobody reads the part which says I give the dough away already. The best one of all was from a guy who sends a postcard. He comes right out and lays his aces on the table. Just send it all to him. No foolin' around, no proposition, no nothing, jes' send him the dirt — all of it.

VIRGINIA

Disgusting.

SETH

Naw, least he was honest.

EATER

Them crummy bastards — always with their hands in somebody else's pocket.

SETH

Yeh — you wouldn't know how to do that, would ya, Eater?

EATER

(*offguard*) Me? 'Course I —

SETH

'Course ya wouldn't.

CRANNIE

(*imitating Seth*) 'Cccourse ya w-wouldn't —

EATER

(*turning savagely on Crannie*) Knock it off, half-wit!

SETH

(*pulling Eater away from Crannie*) So let's have it, Eater. How do you want me to spend the dough I ain't got? What's yer proposition?

EATER

(*sulking*) Na, forget it.

SETH

No no, I wanna hear . . I'm curious.

MINNIE

Spit it out, will ya? He's askin' ya.

EATER

Okay okay — what we wanna do is —

MINNIE

We figger with a little green we can —

EATER

Shut yer graveyard. It's *my* idea, I'll tell it.

MINNIE

Well, unflap yer tongue, will ya? I'm goin' to pieces waitin' for you to say somethin' . .

EATER

It's like this, Seth. Minnie here's a good whore —

MINNIE

I don't like that word, ya son of a bitch.

EATER

All right, all right, yer a lady of the evening, a bale of straw, a swinger, whatever the hell, it's all the same —

MINNIE

It ain't neither. There's a difference, but a slob like you can't be expected to know it.

EATER

(*to Seth*) We been battin' the idea around for a couple of days —

MINNIE

A whore don't give nothin' away free. I give a little love —

EATER

(*in a wild rage*) WILL YOU SHUDDUP, GODDAMN IT TO HELL, BEFORE I KNOCK YA OVER THE HEAD — GODDAMN IT, GODDAMN IT, GODDAMN IT!! (*pounds his head in frustration*)

MINNIE

(*leaping away from him*) Okay okay! Jeesus! Would ya believe we come from the same Ma and Pa?

SETH

Here, Eater, take another drink and get some of the wrinkles outta yer balloon.

EATER

The hell with it. I ain't gonna say it. You can all kiss my ass.

MINNIE

Some treat that'd be.

VIRGINIA

(*stepping up to Seth*) Please, Mr. Hagen, take your money and move out of here — (*Seth grabs Virginia in his arms and waltzes her around.*)

SETH

(*singing and laughing*)

>Money money money, come and be my honey,
>Money money money, you're all very funny,
>Money money money, money money money —

MINNIE

What's such a big deal? Jes' say it, that's all —

CRANNIE

Whyncha ll-let mme s-say it?

EATER

(*plopping down on the ground and holding his head*) Oh shit!

VIRGINIA

Mr. Hagen, you gotta get outta here.

SETH

What for? I like it here. Fresh air, space. Every night I look up and see the Old Man waiting for me with a loaf of bread, a pound of bologna, a smoke, and a bottle of Dago Red. (*to the sky*) Ain't that right, Daddy?

VIRGINIA

But you've got a future now —

SETH

Oh hell, woman, future . . jeez . . we're jes' visitors in life . . we come to stay awhile, look around, and then shove off again. Future! I don't want no four walls closin' me in. I gotta get out and cover with the moon! (*grabs Virginia again*)

>Money money money, it ain't so sunny
>When there's —

VIRGINIA

(*breaking loose*) Stop it! STOP IT! YOU DUMB FOOL! YOU MUST BE CRAZY! (*All activity stops.*) Now you listen to me. My grandmother . . grandmother . . stroke paralyzed her whole right side . . lost her voice . . and for six years my mother nursed her . . worried over her . . and I cursed that old woman . . told her . . told her to die and . . leave my mommy

104

alone . . and my mom . . heard me . . and . . and . . soon after the old woman leaned back in her pillow . . and passed away . . (*begins to break down as the memory overtakes her*) and Virginia's mom never forgave . . never talked to Virginia again . . wouldn't go out . . pulled down the window shades . . and . . oh . . Virginia came home one day and found her on the floor . . right there . . on the floor . . she was . . she was . . dead . . dead . . (*at the crest of the hill*) And like a wild animal, Virginia ran away from that house . . she just ran . . all over the country . . to New York, Houston, Dallas, Chicago, Detroit . .

MINNIE

(*holding her head in agony*) AND ALL POINTS WEST TO THE FRIGGIN' NUTHOUSE!

VIRGINIA

(*jarred back to the present*) House! Yes yes . . the house . . that's what I'm telling you . . get a house for yourself . . get a house . . and . .

EATER

(*jumping in*) That's it . . that's it . . fits right in with what we been trying to say . .

MINNIE

Yeh, Eater, go, go, man —

EATER

(*shoving her away*) Get the hell away! Seth . . Seth, look, look, baby, all we want . .

SETH

Boy, I'm gettin' tired . . look, if I'd taken that dough it'd never be the same with us around here . . c'mon now, lay off . . I ain't got it and that's . .

MINNIE

Yer lyin'!

SETH

(*lookings at her warningly*) Whoops.

EATER

(*shouting*) You got it and you gotta divvy up with us. That's our law and you know it!

SETH

Okay, then search me . . go ahead . . search me!

EATER

(*suddenly shifting gears and throwing his arms around Seth*) Now wait wait wait . . jes' wait wait . . wait a minute . . Now . . it's like I said before . . we gotta stick together, right?

MINNIE

(*also throwing her arms around Seth, with Crannie following suit*) Right. And like you said, Seth, it's a great life, right?

SETH

Did I say that?

CRANNIE

R-rrright.

EATER

Right. Outta sight here . . don't bother nobody . . nobody bother us . . right?

MINNIE and CRANNIE

RIGHT!

EATER

(*they are rocking Seth back and forth*) And . . once . . awhile . . throw out a five bucker 'n a run made for a real big jug. Right?

MINNIE and CRANNIE

RIGHT!

EATER

It's the law, right?

MINNIE

RIGHT RIGHT DOUBLE RIGHT! JEESUS, GET TO THE POINT!

EATER

Shuddup. Piper's law . . we gotta share . . nobody holds out, right?

SETH

(*weak with laughter*) Oh shit.

VIRGINIA

(*trying to get to Seth*) Get away from them, Mr. Hagen!

EATER

(*pushes her away*) Set Minnie up . . got a good motor and more positions 'n a string of Texas whores working full time 'round the clock . .

MINNIE

First come, first serve!

EATER

Put her inna apartment 'r house like Ginny says . .

VIRGINIA

That's not the kind of house I had in mind!

EATER

(*desperate*) Don't matter . . sounds good, huh, Seth?

MINNIE

And pretty soon I add a couple of other sweet-lookin' hookers . . 'n get a bigger place 'n make it a combination gym and pep-up joint for rich johns who want somethin' extra. Legit, see? Everybody stays in shape . .

EATER

(*trying to placate Virginia*) Yeh, and no reason why we can't work you in, too, Virginia . .

VIRGINIA

What?

CRANNIE

Y-yeh . . you c-can ssserve coffee 'n doughnuts . .

MINNIE

Hey, Crannie came up with an idea!

CRANNIE

(*grinning delightedly*) Y-yyyeh!

EATER

How about it, Seth? We all split . . you get more, 'course, becuz yer puttin' up the dinero . . and then we all be livin' *good*, wearin' *good* clothes, eating and drinking *good* . .

CRANNIE

(*going into his traffic cop routine*) And mmme a c-c-cop!

VIRGINIA

(*with surprising strength she pulls Seth away from them*) Don't listen to that crazy talk!

MINNIE

(*her fist cocked*) You shut yer mean mouth, you frigid bitch!

VIRGINIA

They're conning you, Mr. Hagen . . I hope you got the sense . .

EATER

WHATTA YA MEAN? Honest to God . . I jes' told how we all . . we all split . . we . . me, Minnie, Cran . . WE do all the work . . he's jes' gotta get us started . . ain't nobody connin' . . oh, what a shitty thing to say, Miss . . Miss . . Miss . . uh . .

CRANNIE

V-Virginia. (*Eater catches him with a hard slap in the mouth.*)

SETH

(*falling apart with laughter*) Oh man, I'm gonna break a gut — the check — I guess I gotta let ya have it, huh, Eater?

EATER

Yeh, well . . JEESUS . . what the hell ya think . . yeh . . sure . .

SETH

Okay, okay . . (*He gets pencil and paper from a crate.*) "Pay to the order of Eater comma Leftover . . Skinny comma Minnie . . and Juice comma Cranberry . . the sum of twenty comma NAUGHT NAUGHT NAUGHT . .

EATER

(*snatching it out of Seth's hands*) Lemme see, lemme see . . it's to us, all of it . . holy . . yer givin' it all to us!

MINNIE

(*snatching it from Eater*) WOW WOW WOW! (*Seth snatches the check back just as Crannie reaches for it.*)

SETH

I ain't finished . . (*Seth resumes writing something on the paper. Then he hands it to Minnie.*)

MINNIE

(*looking at it*) Ya put down three more naughts.

EATER

(*looking over her shoulder*) Twenty . . MILLION dollars?

SETH

R-r-r-r-right! ALL YERS! (*wheezing with laughter*)

EATER

(*after a stunned beat*) You son of a bitch . . you lousy . . (*He crumples the "check," throws it at Seth, and comes for him. Seth meets him head on and grabs him. They are all very drunk by now.*)

SETH

Pull the grass outta yer ears and point 'em at my mouth. THERE'S . . NO . . CHECK . . BECAUSE . . I . . REJECTED . . THE . . CHECK . . AND . . NOW . . THERE'S . . NO . . CHECK . . TO . . REJECT . . GET IT? (*He pushes Eater away and does a crazy little jig.*)

The check, the check, no check to reject,
Reject, reject, what check to reject?

(*He falls down. Virginia runs to help him up.*)

EATER

YA PUT IT AWAY!

SETH

Where away, ya horse's ass?

MINNIE

Ya hid it around here someplace.

SETH

Then look for it. Tear up the joint . .

EATER

This is business, goddamn it . .

ANNIVERSARY ON WEEDY HILL

SETH

Business my shiny pink ass . . don't wanna own nothin' . . got nothin'
and nothin' standin' in the way . . 'at's what we got . . but it's better'n
that . . out there . . (*pointing to the freeway*) maniacs . . inhale ya up
one side of their nose 'n blow ya out the other . . hack ya to pieces . . human
bein's ain't been invented . . World War Forever . .

EATER

He's flippin' . .

SETH

. . 'round it goes! Greedy greedy lil pals . . grab a sucker by the hair
and cover yer balls . . world . . lissen WORLD . . YOU GOT NOTHIN' I
WANT . . I HATE YOU . . HAAAAAAAATE YOUUUUUUUUUU
. . SMEAR YER GODDAMN FREEWAYS WITH YER FAT BLOOD . . YOU . .
YOU SCREW-FACED SUCKED-UP ZOMBIES . . YOU . . YOU . . AAAAAARGH
. . GARRRRRRRRAH . . RRRRRRRRAUGH . . (*His rage sputters into wild
facial grimaces and a variety of animal sounds.*)

EATER

(*to his confederates*) C'MON, MOVE! HE'S OUT OF IT . . MOVE . . LOOK
FOR THE DOUGH . . IT'S AROUND HERE SOMEPLACE . . TEAR UP THE JOINT
. . FIND IT!! (*Eater, Minnie, and Crannie fly into a hurricane of action.
Eater turns furniture over, tearing apart whatever he can. Minnie smashes
Seth's dolls apart, looking for the elusive check. Crannie is simply having
a ball, throwing papers and debris into the air.*)

SETH

(*subsiding but not yet aware of what's going on*) No more . . no more
. . they'll all be up here someday . . wait . . jes' wait . . yes-
sir . . nothin' but Weedy Hills all over the world . . (*Virginia has gotten
into a wildcat fight with Minnie when she tries to interfere with what the
latter is doing. Eater pulls Minnie off.*)

EATER

No time for fightin', crissakes . . (*They resume their destruction of Seth's
"house."*)

SETH

(*coming out of his stupor*) Hey hey, whatta ya doin'? (*He runs from one
to the other.*) Minnie, hey . . my toys . . don't . .

VIRGINIA

For god's sake, get out of here . . run for your life!

SETH

(*brushing her off*) Minnie, leave my toys alone . . lissen to me . .

VIRGINIA

(*hanging onto him*) I don't want any of it . . keep it for yourself . .

SETH

(*trying to grab Crannie*) Crannie, Crannie . . stop that . .

VIRGINIA

All I want dear god is sleep . . had all the noise a body could wish for . .

SETH

(*angrily pushing her aside*) GET AWAY! EATER, GODDAMN YOU, LEAVE MY FURNITURE ALONE!

VIRGINIA

Please, please, take your money and run, run, run . .

SETH

(*enraged, he knocks her to the ground*) GET THE HELL OUTTA HERE, YOU BEDEVILED LEECH! YOU WORSE THAN THESE NUT-TWIDDLERS . . WHO DO I TRUST AROUND HERE? GODALMIGHTY . . TRUST . . FROM SOMEBODY, YOU STOMPED-ON BITCHBUM!! (*Dazed, Virginia crawls away from him. Eater, Minnie, and Crannie have exhausted their frantic search, leaving the place a shambles.*)

EATER

Son of a bitch, son of a bitch, son of a bitch . . (*Virginia gets up and runs off the hill. It's the last we see of her.*)

SETH

(*staggering toward the hill*) GINNY . . GINNY . . YOU ALLEY-WHORE . . COME BACK . . WAIT . . I DIDN'T MEAN . . GINNY . . DON'T RUN AWAY . . I LOVE YOU . . GINNY . . (*Exhausted, he falls to his knees.*) Happy Anniversary, Seth ol' fathead . . here's to ol' Seth on Fathead Hill . . (*Minnie suddenly lurches at him with a screwdriver in her hands, murder in her heart. Crannie sees her and screams.*)

CRANNIE

AAAH! AAAH! AAAAH!

MINNIE

(*whirling around*) Whatta ya yellin', ya feeble-minded — (*She goes for Crannie with the screwdriver.*)

EATER

(*grabbing her*) Knock it off . . all ya got in yer head is screwin' and stickin' things in people . .

MINNIE

(*hysterically*) He had no right . . no right . . was ours as much as his . .

SETH

I didn't want to lose what we got, Minnie . .

EATER

What the hell we got?

ANNIVERSARY ON WEEDY HILL

SETH

(*after a beat*) Time.

EATER

Huh?

SETH

The loot would put us back in the ring, Eater . . and . . we jes' ain't got the legs for it no more . .

EATER

Bughouse.

SETH

Maybe . . maybe . . that's . . matter of opinion . . but one day a long time ago . . (*at the crest of the hill, his form outlined against the fading sky*) I said out loud to myself, "Take yer ass in yer two good hands and get out, Seth, boy. Get down to *nothin'* and live under a tree, near a river, or on the side of a weedy hill — any place where you can stretch out yer arms and catch yer breath." I thought you all felt the same way. (*They stare silently at him.*) Aw, what'd I do to Ginny? (*He stares out in the direction she left.*) Ginny . . Miss . . Ginny . . (*tries to pull himself together*) 'Sallright, 'sallright, she'll be back . . always comes back . . c'mon . . we're still buddies . . we all got the same 'n we're all buddies . . bud-*dies*, right, Eater, right? (*Laughing, he looks around at the group. They just stare at him steadily. Even Crannie seems to have gone into a trance.*) Huh? Hey, what's the matter . . what'd ya . . jeesus . . say somethin' . . migod . . you know what ya . . ya . . christ . . ya look jes' like some of . . (*Without taking their eyes off him, the group rises and moves slowly toward him. The sky grows darker.*) Oh, I get, I get it! (*laughing hysterically*) You crazy bastards! Yer tryin' to RAT ME! You half-wits, you can't do that . . (*They have him encircled now. Seth suddenly relaxes and offers himself to the "execution." The trio drops its tension for a second. Then suddenly Eater's hands fly out and seize Seth by the neck. Minnie follows suit, but Cranberry panics and backs away. Seth struggles but can't free himself from the fury of the insane. Finally he goes limp and slides lifeless to the ground. Cranberry, whimpering, runs offstage. Eater and Minnie dazedly follow him. The sky darkens.*)

THE END

Anniversary on Weedy Hill by Allen Joseph was presented June 12, 1970, at the Theatre West/Club Theatre, Los Angeles. It was directed by Jerome Guardino.

Cast of Characters

SETH HAGEN	Sam Gilman
VIRGINIA	Betty Garrett
MINNIE SKINNY	Ann Morgan Guilbert
LEFTOVER EATER	Guy Raymond
CRANBERRY JUICE	Hal Lynch

WILLIAM N. MONSON

The Nihilist

PLAYWRIGHT'S NOTE

Sergei Nechaev was an actual revolutionary. The events he describes in the play did happen — but not necessarily as he relates them. And that should be remembered: this is Nechaev's play. It reflects the drive and turmoil of his mind, and any production should reinforce this point. He is narrator, ringmaster, hero, and the play is pervaded by the real Nechaev's sense of melodrama and sardonic humor. To a certain extent, all of the events and characters are thus Nechaev's creations; they exist as he desires them to be — and this forces some of them close to stereotypes. But reality does intrude: both Trepov and the Major successfully break Nechaev's control of the play. On a psychological level, they might be said to be Nechaev's "conscience" letting the truth be known or his doubts finding expression. On a more practical level, they represent a deliberate device on *my* part to jar the audience into realizing that most of the play is Nechaev's version of "truth" and to place objectivity in opposition to the general subjective approach of the play.

This conflict necessitates considerable range in the manner of production. Some scenes are representational, some stylized (like the third court scene), some shatter completely the illusion (like Trepov's struggle to be more than a stereotype and the Major's arrest scene), and Nechaev often addresses the audience directly. The desired result of such deliberate juxtaposition is an audience both emotionally and intellectually involved. The "truth" of the story then becomes a riddle — to be sought out and solved amidst Nechaev's web of deception.

There can be considerable freedom in designing and directing a production of this play. Suggestions are given for a multimedia approach, but the play can be done without using them. The set can be multileveled and complex, with flying flats — or simple, depending heavily upon lighting and/or projected scenery. The cast can be large with many extras or smaller with projected crowds and crowd sounds and actors doubling and tripling. Masks might even be used for some of the characters. Nechaev should have a spotlight in which to address the audience. The Ten Demands should be passed out to the audience on poorly printed stock as in the Optional Prologue or as part of the program. For reference purposes, the Revolutionary Catechism may be found in several books, such as Robert Payne's *Life and Death of Lenin.*

Whatever production choices are made, the director should seek his unity within Nechaev's mind, molding the play to his vision of what Nechaev means. How much, for example, does Nechaev *lie*? And be warned: there is comedy here, and melodrama. Nechaev has a strong sense of parody but he is not above dramatizing himself seriously. The laughter and shock and hamminess of the story he tells should combine to give a powerful portrait of the man's mind. And when the audience leaves at the play's conclusion, they should feel they have experienced not only a few dramatic moments in history but the impact of a revolutionary mind.

Cast of Characters

The Revolutionaries

SERGEI NECHAEV, the nihilist

VERA ZASNER, female socialist; Tkachev's "wife"

PETER TKACHEV, early leader; a Hertzen populist

SOFIA PEROVNA, female terrorist; Drovnik's mistress

ANDREI DROVNIK, Nechaev's protégé; later leader

NICKOLAY KIBALCHICH, scholar-bomber

IVAN PRIZHOV, destitute author and hanger-on

DMITRI KUZNETSOV, bookstore clerk and fringe member

IVAN IVANOVICH IVANOV, Moscow group leader

ALEXANDER HERTZEN, socialist pioneer; founder of populism

NATALIE HERTZEN, his daughter

MIKHAIL BAKUNIN, early socialist and nihilist

NICKOLAY OGAREV, poet, aging propagandist

ALEXANDER ULYANOV, a late convert

VLADIMIR ULYANOV, Alexander's younger brother, later Lenin

Their Sympathizers

DUKE URUSOV, lawyer and liberal reformer

THE CORPORAL, Nechaev's guard in the Ravelin

OTHER STUDENTS   TOWNSPEOPLE

Their Opponents

THE MAJOR, of the Third Division secret police

GENERAL TREPOV, chief of police

THE CHANCELLOR, of St. Petersburg University

THE JUDGE   THE PROSECUTOR

AN ORTHODOX PRIEST   FOUR POLICEMEN

A DRUMMER

(NOTE. Considerable doubling is possible, especially among the minor roles and for crowd scenes.)

THE NIHILIST

ACT ONE

Optional Prologue

The play may begin even as the audience enters, with the cast demon-strating in the lobby or on the sidewalk outside the theatre. They can carry picket signs (End Government Tyranny, No More Stupid Wars, Students Demand Freedom, Revolution Is the Answer, etc.) and they can distribute the Ten Demands to the patrons as they enter:

Ten Demands!!!

The Community of Students makes the following demands upon the Administration:

1. The Administration must remove *all* military aspects from the curriculum and campus life!
2. Students must have the right to wear the clothes we choose! The student body is composed of people from many differ-ent cultural heritages. We must be allowed to dress as we please!
3. Students have the right to wear our hair as long as we like and in any fashion we like! There must be *no* rules about hair length or hair styles!
4. The Administration must relinquish control over extracur-ricular activities! We are *adults* and must be treated as such!
5. Students must have the right to organize our own lectures, concerts, and theatre performances! We must be allowed

the speakers, musicians, and plays *we* like — without interference or censorship!

6. Scholarships must be administered by fair, impartial juries of *students and teachers* — free from harassment by Administration bureaucrats!

7. Students must have the right to form ethnic groups and clubs! We are a community of *many* races and origins. We want to recognize them and allow them identity! *We will not be conformed!!*

8. Students must have the right to install and manage *our own* eating facilities and select *our own* food! The food here is fit only for *pigs*!!

9. Money *must* be provided for student relief funds! State scholarship and financial programs must be turned over to the Community of Students!

10. The Community of Students must administer these funds *without Administration interference*!

These demands are *non-negotiable* and must be granted TODAY!!

The Community of Students Committee

Since the costumes of Russia circa 1870 parallel today's student fetishes, the advantage in using the prologue is to establish a direct parallel or blur in time. Nothing should be said or done to indicate the period of the play until Nechaev reveals it. (A similar result may be achieved with the onstage opening, but the sidewalk prologue is an interesting alternative.) All the conspirators except Nechaev should take part in this. He should remain free and somewhat aloof from it, moving at will and playing his recorder. All should wear scarves or armbands of tricolor symbolizing their revolutionary sympathies. At curtain time, the actors may then move into the theatre as a group, beginning their shouting outside — perhaps "All ten now!" Then they should move down the aisles, toward the stage, confronting the audience, and finally move up onto the stage to begin their cry for the Chancellor.

Scene 1

If the play begins onstage, Nechaev's recorder (called flute in the play) should be heard in the darkness after the houselights dim. Then the stage lights should come up to reveal him sitting high on the set, playing. He stops, looks at the audience, smiles in amusement, and makes a gesture of command. Immediately, the demonstrators begin shouting offstage, then boil into view. Nechaev cavorts above them, using the recorder as a baton as he leads their chanting with Tkachev. The major characters are the follow-

THE NIHILIST

ing: Sergei Nechaev, a young man in his early twenties, not handsome and plainly dressed, but with an intensity and catlike grace which make him resemble a stalking animal at times. Peter Nikitich Tkachev, a tall, slender, introspective man in his late twenties, once a journalist, now an agitator. Vera Zasner, a young woman in her late teens or early twenties, not unattractive, an idealist and romanticist, intensely dedicated to whatever cause she follows. Sofia Perovna, a short-haired woman in her mid-twenties who wears peasant boots and masculine clothes with little blue eyeglasses. An intense and dedicated revolutionary. Ivan Ivanov, a petulant man in his early twenties, perhaps with gold-rimmed glasses and moustache. Like Tkachev, he is the son of a nobleman turned to agitation. Dmitri Kuznetsov, a very nervous, somewhat effeminate man in his early twenties; a disinherited nobleman now a bookstore clerk, seeking salvation in revolution. Ivan Prizhov, a balding, undisciplined hanger-on in his late forties, nearly destitute, poorly dressed, dirty, with ragged beard and moustache. Loud and vulgar but not unlikable. The demonstrators are in good spirits, and there is much clowning, slogan-shouting, and ad-libbed interplay. The stage is now the University. Three other students wander in. (Later, they will appear as Kibalchich, Drovnik, and Ulyanov.) They stand watching. Duke Urusov enters briskly. He is well dressed, wears a neatly trimmed beard, and perhaps carries a walking stick. He is a well-known liberal lawyer and favorable toward the demonstration, nodding to the marchers who greet him as they pass. Slipping in almost unnoticed is the Major, a plainclothes officer of the Third Division, the Czar's secret police. He is gray, nearing fifty, and wears rumpled clothes. Though somewhat nearsighted, he uses his gold-rimmed eyeglasses (carried in a pocket case) only to read. Across his vest is a gold chain for a pocket watch he periodically consults and winds, and he is a constant pipe smoker. A good-humored, gentle individual but one who can be tough and steel-hard in his dedication to his work. Now, he lights his pipe and watches the demonstration with some amusement. Ivanov and Tkachev move up beside Nechaev and begin chanting: "We want the Chancellor, we want the Chancellor!" *The others quickly pick up the chant and shout it until he appears. The Chancellor is a gray, stocky man, pompous and important. He raises his hands as he stands high on the ramparts above them, and the chanting dies away.*

CHANCELLOR

I have a statement. (*reads*) "The Board of Governors of this University has met in special session to consider your proposals."

IVANOV

Demands!

WILLIAM N. MONSON

CHANCELLOR

"After careful discussion, they have consented to grant numbers 2, 3, 7, and 8 concerning clothes, hair length, ethnic groups, and eating facilities." (*The crowd cheers.*) "As to the other requests . ."

IVANOV

Demands! We demand them!

CHANCELLOR

"As to the others . . although money cannot be allocated for student relief funds administered by students, additional money will be sought for scholarships and student aid, to be administered by the University. A plan for possible reorganization of the Scholarship Board will be considered at our next regular meeting. The Board makes these grants in the spirit of progress and good will, and it hopes you will accept them in the same spirit."

TKACHEV

What about Number 1? What about the military?

IVANOV

And control of extracurricular activities?

CHANCELLOR

The University will never relinquish its right to establish curriculum and practices. Nor will it give up its control over University-connected activities.

TKACHEV

And who decides what they are?

CHANCELLOR

We do. The Board of Governors and I.

CROWD

(*various*) No! No! We're the University, too!

SOFIA

What about the student you expelled?

CHANCELLOR

He was expelled because he broke University regulations.

IVANOV

He was expelled because his hair was too long and he didn't think and act the way you wanted him to.

CHANCELLOR

He was insubordinate to a professor and refused to conform to University rules. This institution must have order and discipline or it will cease to serve its purpose.

TKACHEV

Its purpose is to turn out conformists. We will not be conformed. We want freedom!

THE NIHILIST

CROWD

(*various*) Freedom! Freedom!

CHANCELLOR

Why do you act this way? You have greater freedom now than ever before. (*The crowd hoots and boos.*) It's true. Oh, I know these are difficult times for all of us. Our classrooms are crowded. There isn't enough money to pay for all the students who want an education. But we are doing the best we can. And you should respect us for that.

CROWD

(*hoots, laughs, various catcalls*) Is this your best? You can do better than this. We'll never respect your kind.

TKACHEV

If you want our respect, earn it. Prove how enlightened you are. Give amnesty to those you've expelled and grant all ten of our demands.

CHANCELLOR

That's beyond my power. I've done all that I can do.

IVANOV

We can do more! We can close down this University!

NECHAEV

(*leading*) Strike, strike, strike!

CROWD

(*picks up chant*) Strike, strike, strike! (*The Chancellor gestures for quiet, but Ivanov and Tkachev urge on the crowd, and the Chancellor finally gives up in disgust, makes an angry gesture, and leaves. The crowd roars at this and chants even louder. Nechaev suddenly flings up his arms. Everyone onstage freezes, except for the Major who stands nearly motionless, watching. Cyclorama: a large slide of Nechaev, a grinning, triumphant Nechaev. Each time this image appears, it should be larger — or more of a closeup — until at the play's end it is gigantic. Nechaev looks around, chuckles, and strolls down to the audience.*)

NECHAEV

Sound familiar? Well, I have a surprise for you. This is St. Petersburg University, 1869. (*laughs*) Let me introduce myself. I am Sergei Nechaev, the nihilist, and like Jesus — the son of a carpenter. Like the Nazarene, I also teach religion. I'm sort of a revolutionary rabbi. (*laughs*) This is my story, my play. You are here tonight to be catechized, and I am your catechist. Everything you will see actually happened. I am real and so are they. (*indicates others*) So are all the events which will occur. Oh, I've doctored them slightly so you can see them all in one evening, but their context is complete. I have lots of fun for you tonight — sex, violence, all those things you really enjoy. There will also be some things you won't like — but then . . that's the point. Now, settle back — if you can. (*announcing*) Act One — the Rise of the Messiah. (*Nechaev makes another gesture with his arms; the slide disappears, and the chant of "Strike!" resumes, continuing until Tkachev climbs to the top of the ramparts and gestures for quiet.*)

TKACHEV

Students! People of St. Petersburg! The cause we labor for today is more than ten demands. More than the injustice of an expelled brother. It is the cause of free men everywhere. (*indicates his scarf*) It began with the French Revolution. Our French comrades knew how to deal with a decadent society. The People arose and ended the aristocracy. (*The crowd cheers and there are cries of* "Down with the aristocracy.") And what happened in Mother Russia as this wave of the future swelled in the west? Our monarchs tried to keep us ignorant of it — to suppress all mention of freedom and democracy — and imprisoned those who spoke of them.

But a beacon of hope now pierced the gloom of oppression, and brave men followed that lonely light: Hertzen, Ogarev, Petrashevsky, Mikhailov. They wrote about freedom. They fought for it. They are in prison or exile today because of it. But what little we enjoy, they helped win for us. Can we do any less for our children?

CROWD

No! (*chanting*) Freedom, justice! (*Ivanov, his eyes bright and wild, climbs up and shoulders Tkachev aside. He waves his hands for quiet.*)

IVANOV

I am Ivanov. I come from Moscow where we share your concern about freedom and justice. (*This interests the Major who takes out a little book and makes notes during the following speech.*) I lead a group there which battles against tyranny, and I am here today to urge you to form a group in St. Petersburg — to join us in a great brotherhood. We must complete the work begun by those who went before. This protest is only the beginning. We must unite to save our country from its tyrants. (*pauses for effect; then*) It has been eight years since our Czar Alexander freed the serfs. We called him "Emancipator" then, but are the serfs really free?

CROWD

No!

IVANOV

They are still helpless, tied to the land. Barely better off than before. And what happened when we tried to protest? The "Great Emancipator" had us jailed — and flogged — and exiled!

CROWD

(*various*) Tyrant! Oppressor! Down with tyranny!

THE NIHILIST

IVANOV

But the People will not give in. This city has burned before with our anger. It can burn again!

CROWD

(*various*) Yes. Burn it! Burn it!

IVANOV

And no Romanoff is safe in its streets. They tried to kill the Grand Duke Constantine and even shot at the Czar himself.

CROWD

(*various*) Yes, yes, yes! (*Cyclorama: slide — Alexander II stares down at Ivanov.*)

IVANOV

Hear me, Alexander. There are others who will turn to fire and knives and guns and bombs if reason does not change you. Listen, oh Czar. The wave is cresting. You must change your ways. You must change them now. Grant us freedom before it costs you your life!

CROWD

(*roars with approval, then chants*) Down with the Czar! (*As the chant swells, police whistles suddenly sound nearby, and General Trepov and several policemen — at least four — rush onto the stage. Trepov is an energetic man in his forties, bearded, something of a dandy, who wears a quasi-military uniform and highly polished boots in his job as chief of police. He has a pistol in a holster but does not use it as he directs the breaking up of the demonstration. The policemen are various ages and wear drab, quasi-military uniforms. They carry clubs or rubber truncheons which they use with vigor on the demonstrators, driving them off the stage. They carefully avoid the Duke and the Major, who calmly surveys the violence swirling around him, notebook still in hand. Nechaev helps Vera hide in one of the blind corners of the set. Kuznetsov is clubbed down, screaming, but rescued by Ivanov and Sofia who get him safely offstage. Finally, only the Major, the Duke, and Trepov are left onstage with the policemen, who stand catching their breath or on guard about the stage. Trepov crosses to where the Duke regards him with revulsion. The Major sits on a step and tries to decipher his notes during the following.*)

TREPOV

(*to his men*) Well done. They'll remember this day for a while.

DUKE

(*bitterly*) So will others.

TREPOV

We've met before. Duke Urusov, isn't it? Lawyer and liberal.

DUKE

(*a stiff bow*) General Trepov. Does the chief of police always take part in such work as this?

TREPOV

When it gives him satisfaction.

DUKE

You're a sadist. You didn't have to club them.

TREPOV

(*toying with him*) They would have been disappointed if we hadn't. They'd feel we let them down. Didn't live up to our reputation. Besides, in the perverse way of revolutionaries, they enjoy being clubbed. It gives them a feeling of importance, of martyrdom.

DUKE

And you enjoy it, too, don't you?

TREPOV

I like to see my men enjoying themselves. This keeps them in practice.

DUKE

You're an animal.

TREPOV

I'm a man who deals with animals. You don't trade talk with a jackass. If he balks, you beat him.

DUKE

In that case, General, I have no further words to trade with you. Good day. (*The Duke turns and exits — white with shock and fury. Disgruntled by the Duke's parting remark, Trepov turns his sarcasm on the Major, who has taken out his glasses now to read his notes.*)

TREPOV

Well, did the illustrious Third Division find anything new to interest them today?

MAJOR

Perhaps. I'll have to do some more checking. (*puts away his notebook and glasses*) I'll need two of your men to help me.

TREPOV

For what?

MAJOR

(*quietly*) I'm sorry, General. You know I can't tell you.

TREPOV

(*he's heard this before*) Why not? We both work for the government. We're supposed to be on the same side.

MAJOR

But you work for the minister of the interior, and the Third Division is responsible only to the Czar and his Chancery. Whatever I find out has to be sent to you through the regular channels.

TREPOV

Channels! High and mighty secret police. The Czar's pets. You should be working for me. I'd see to it you got better results.

MAJOR

(*stung*) We get results enough to please the Czar.

TREPOV

Alexander is far too lenient.

MAJOR

Perhaps . . May I have those two men and get on with my work?

TREPOV

And if I say no?

MAJOR

(*shrugs*) It would have to be reported.

TREPOV

(*a snarl*) Take them and be damned! (*They bow to each other and part. The Major takes two policemen off in one direction; Trepov leads the others off in another. When they have gone, Nechaev helps Vera out of hiding.*)

NECHAEV

It's safe now. They've gone. I'll see you home.

VERA

(*uneasily*) All right. (*a pause, then*) I want to thank you for what you did.

NECHAEV

(*taking her hands*) How?

VERA

(*uneasily*) Nechaev . . ! (*She tries to pull her hands free, but Nechaev holds them more firmly, looking at them.*)

NECHAEV

You have nice hands. A noblewoman's hands. They would feel good on a man's back. (*He confronts her squarely, putting the hands on his chest, pulling her closer.*)

VERA

(*half-pleading*) I'm Tkachev's wife.

NECHAEV

In name only. (*They look at each other for a long moment. She is weakening to his hypnotic stare. Just in time, Tkachev runs in, and Nechaev frees her.*)

TKACHEV

Vera! Thank God you're safe. (*They embrace.*)

NECHAEV

Thank Nechaev, not God.

VERA

Nechaev helped me escape.

NECHAEV

(*pointedly to Tkachev*) Where were *you*?

TKACHEV

(*bristling*) Come along, Vera. We'd better get back to our room. The others will be gathering. (*to Nechaev*) You keep watch at the street door until they all arrive. (*Nechaev doesn't like this, but Tkachev takes Vera toward the Uburnov room before he can complain. Nechaev steps down to the audience.*)

NECHAEV

(*to the audience*) The "husband" is Peter Tkachev, a liberal reformer and writer. Our demonstration today was his idea. The "wife" is Vera Zasner, daughter of a forestry official in Smolensk. They're living together on her inheritance under the name of "Uburnov." He claims it's a matter of a convenience. Hah! (*Vera and Tkachev have entered the Uburnov room, which is located on a higher level and contains a bed, a small table, two chairs, perhaps a bookcase with a few books. There are posters of Hertzen, Ogarev, and Bakunin on the walls. Vera lights the candle on the table, then sets out a bottle of wine, glasses, some bread, and a bread knife. She begins to cut the bread as Tkachev consults a book.*) He's looking for answers to our problems in that book. Since it was written by Alexander Hertzen, he won't find them. (*Ivanov enters with Sofia and Kuznetsov, who has a bandage around his head and looks as if he has been crying.*) Well, fugitives. Where have you been hiding?

IVANOV

In an infirmary. We took Kuznetsov to get his head mended.

KUZNETSOV

(*whimpering*) They took seven stitches!

SOFIA

We know. You screamed on every one.

NECHAEV

Vera and Tkachev are waiting for you upstairs. We're going to conduct an autopsy on our demonstration. (*at Ivanov*) I think we'll find the cause of death was foolhardy rhetoric.

IVANOV

(*bristles, then*) I see you've finally found your place in life. As a doorman. (*flips him a coin*) For your services. (*Ivanov wheels and starts in. Sofia and Kuznetsov follow.*)

THE NIHILIST

NECHAEV

(*seething*) Beware, Ivan Ivanov. (*The others continue on, but Ivanov cannot resist turning for one more riposte. He nods stiffly and clicks his heels.*)

IVANOV

Ivan Ivanovich Ivanov. (*He turns and follows Sofia and Kuznetsov up to the room.*)

NECHAEV

(*to the audience*) His father had a hard time with names. The arrogant bastard is the son of a nobleman and won't let anyone forget it. He runs a student group of his own in Moscow, but I think he has higher ambitions. (*Vera serves wine to the three of them. Sofia takes a cigarette from a cigarette case and lights it from the candle.*) The daring woman with the cigarette is Sofia Perovna. Don't let her rough peasant looks fool you. Her father was the governor general of St. Petersburg. When he refused to mistreat the student marchers in 1861, he was retired in disgrace. That's when Sofia joined our cause. She's already spent six months in jail for civil disturbances. Don't be fooled by her masculine clothes, either. She's very good in bed. (*He laughs. Kuznetsov petulantly gestures with his own cigarette for a light, and Sofia holds the candle for him to light it.*) That's Dmitri Kuznetsov. He'd like to be good in bed, too. Only he hasn't figured out yet which sex he is. He claims to be the son of a nobleman, but his ancestry is also in question. So his father disowned him, and he works in a bookstore with this toper. (*Nechaev points to Prizhov entering with a bottle.*) Ivan Prizhov, middle-aged hack. Where have you been?

PRIZHOV

I stopped to pick up a friend. (*pats bottle*) And I'm not a hack — I'm a historian.

NECHAEV

Of Russian taverns.

PRIZHOV

The critics gave my book good reviews.

NECHAEV

Of course. You did so much research. (*They laugh and Nechaev takes a pull from the bottle. Prizhov looks up at the room at Vera as she pulls Tkachev out of his book and gives him wine.*)

PRIZHOV

I wish I had a lady like that keeping me.

NECHAEV

You old lecher, you're pea-green with envy.

PRIZHOV

Why, I haven't peed green in years. (*Laughing, they go up to the room.*

As they go in Prizhov speaks.) Too much vodka. Makes you piss yellow. *(As he and Nechaev laugh at this, Tkachev is offended.)*

TKACHEV

I won't have that language around Vera.

NECHAEV

Don't be stuffy. Prizhov can't help it. He's lived all his life with barflies and whores. They like his humor.

TKACHEV

I don't. So stop it.

NECHAEV

(scornfully) This from the man who wants to take Hertzen's advice to "go to the People." Well, here we are, Peter. Prizhov and I are the People.

IVANOV

(snorting) Sons of serfs.

NECHAEV

Exactly. And you two being nobility gone sour, you don't understand us. Nor like us. *(to Tkachev)* But you have to — or you're no disciple of Hertzen's.

PRIZHOV

What does Hertzen know about the poor? He's rich. The rich can afford to be upset about the poor — but they won't live with them.

TKACHEV

Russia's strength comes from the People. Any revolution must begin with them.

NECHAEV

Balls! Revolutions begin with men like us — malcontents. Men who want something — and set out to get it.

TKACHEV

We're not grabbers. We're reformers. Social educators.

NECHAEV

Is that why you gave us that history lesson today? To educate us? "A beacon of hope in the gloom of oppression . . " Shit!

TKACHEV

Nechaev! Your language is as bad as Prizhov's.

PRIZHOV

It's better than yours. You talk like a goddamned textbook.

NECHAEV

We need a leader who talks the People's language.

IVANOV

Meaning you? *(snorts)* You're better suited to be a court jester.

THE NIHILIST

KUZNETSOV

Yes, you can tootle your flute — and lead chants.

NECHAEV

I'm not the fool here. (*at Tkachev*) It's those who think they're revolutionaries — but don't have the stomach for it. (*to Ivanov*) Or the brains. Like today.

PRIZHOV

Our demonstration wasn't exactly a roaring success.

VERA

We made too many mistakes. We've got to agree on our tactics.

TKACHEV

She's right. Ivan, why did you try to take over? It was your threats against the Czar that brought the police down on us.

IVANOV

I said what had to be said. I've given up on these policies of Hertzen which you cherish.

SOFIA

For once, I agree with Ivanov. Peaceful petitions don't work.

VERA

But violence only brings more violence. (*indicates poster*) Remember what Ogarev said —

NECHAEV

Ogarev is a hopelessly romantic poet.

PRIZHOV

And these days, even he leans a bit toward Bakunin. (*indicates poster*)

TKACHEV

I won't let this group follow the lunacies of that anarchist.

NECHAEV

Bakunin rivals Marx as a leader of the world Revolution.

SOFIA

Hertzen has been discredited.

PRIZHOV

A rich man theorizing about the poor. Like a horse telling a hen how to lay eggs. (*All but Vera and Tkachev chorus assent.*)

VERA

(*interceding*) Please! Please! This way, we won't get anywhere.

IVANOV

(*cynically*) What do *you* propose we do?

VERA

We're entirely too unstructured. We need an organization, a plan of operations.

127

IVANOV

Brilliant! Exactly the kind of observation I'd expect from a dilettante.

TKACHEV

That's unfair. Vera may be new to our movement, but she's no dilettante. Furthermore, she's right. We can't go on making plans day to day — changing them as we go, haggling, wasting time. If we're to get anywhere, we need over-all goals and procedures. (*There is general approval for this, but Ivanov is still dubious.*)

IVANOV

And who decides what they are?

VERA

Why not a steering committee — three or four of us. We could draw up a constitution and —

IVANOV

(*interrupting*) Constitution! That's an absurdity. Look at us — part nobility, part serf, part God-knows-what. The only way to make anything of this group is to have the right kind of leader.

SOFIA

Meaning you.

IVANOV

My group in Moscow does quite nicely.

TKACHEV

And now you want to expand into a nationwide organization.

IVANOV

Of course. That's why I'm here. To link your group to mine and the one in Kazan. To show you the way to success.

VERA

(*indicating Kuznetsov's head*) Here's your success. Seven stitches' worth.

IVANOV

Kuznetsov is willing to pay the price for revolution. (*Kuznetsov — the martyr — nods too firmly and the violent movement hurts his head. In the snickers that follow his reaction, Nechaev moves forward.*)

NECHAEV

Horseshit! You don't even know what you're talking about. You organize a group of students into a secret society, and you think you're a revolutionary. All of you are about as dangerous as a group of schoolgirls discussing socialism over Sunday tea.

IVANOV

I know what I'm doing.

NECHAEV

Really? Then why did you use your real name when you made your big speech today? When you tried to take over *our* demonstration! Any fool knows enough to use an alias. (*indicates Tkachev, Sofia, and himself*) Niki, Sonia, Petrovich . . we all use them. But not you, Ivan-Three. You shout your glorious name to the world. By now, the Third Division has a file card on you — and you've jeopardized us all.

KUZNETSOV

I did see a man taking notes of your speech.

PRIZHOV

Only the Third Division does that.

SOFIA

No one else would want to.

NECHAEV

(*to group*) This pompous windbag sees revolution as a tool for his vanity. He doesn't care what it means — only what he gets out of it. He sees himself as a new Danton. Danton from the River Don.

IVANOV

(*applauding*) Very good. Very good. A remarkable metaphor, Nechaev — from a man who taught himself how to read and write.

PRIZHOV

You arrogant snob!

IVANOV

Drunken peasant lout!

NECHAEV

Better a serf than a half-assed aristocrat!

KUZNETSOV

You hate us because we're sons of nobility and were born in good homes. You hate the world because you were born out behind the pigsty.

NECHAEV

But I grew into a man. (*closing on Kuznetsov*) The way I hear it, your noble father threw you out on your noble ear because you lack noble nuts! (*To punctuate this, Nechaev pokes Kuznetsov in the groin, and Kuznetsov backs away, whimpering, holding himself. Sofia joins Prizhov's and Nechaev's laughter.*)

VERA

(*shouting*) Stop it! Stop it! Are we serious about this or not? If we are, we have to forget our backgrounds, our petty differences. How can we unite our country if we're not united ourselves.

IVANOV

The new Joan of Lorraine. And Nechaev, her capering *clown* prince. Are such as you to determine the fate of Russia?

NECHAEV

Beware, Ivan-Three, that I do not determine yours! (*They glare at each other, close to violence. Tkachev steps in.*)

TKACHEV

Stop it, both of you. (*They relax a little.*) Now, we've got to decide what we're going to do next.

NECHAEV

More talk . . ! (*Disgusted, he crosses to the window and looks out. The Major and two policemen have entered the now darkened stage below and are searching the street with lanterns, looking for the right house. Nechaev quickly turns to the others.*)

TKACHEV

I'd like to discuss the idea of a constitution . .

NECHAEV

There won't be time. There are police searching the street.

IVANOV

(*suddenly frightened*) Are they looking for us?

NECHAEV

Who else? You did everything but give them our address.

SOFIA

(*to Tkachev*) What shall we do?

TKACHEV

(*panicked*) I don't know.

NECHAEV

Of course you don't. And by the time you make up your mind, you'll be in jail. (*taking command*) Sofia, Prizhov, Kuznetsov. Across the roof. Don't let them see you. (*to Vera*) Get those posters down. Put them under the covers of the bed. (*Sofia and Prizhov exit through the window, pulling a frightened Kuznetsov along with them. Tkachev helps Vera take down the posters and hide them in the bed. Nechaev puts out the wall lamp, leaving the candle burning on the table.*)

IVANOV

(*frightened*) What about me?

NECHAEV

You and Tkachev will go in a moment.

TKACHEV

You take him. I'm staying with Vera.

NECHAEV

It's you and Ivanov the police are after. Not court jesters. Go — *now!* (*Tkachev unhappily hugs Vera, then follows Ivanov through the window and across the roof. Nechaev looks quickly around, carries the candle to the bed, and begins undressing. Vera looks at him in amazement.*) Get undressed and into bed. Hurry! (*She begins to disrobe, and Nechaev blows out the candle; the room is unlighted for a few moments. Then, there is a commotion, and lanterns illuminate the area as the Major and two policemen enter the room. The lanterns reveal Nechaev and Vera embracing in bed. Vera screams and pulls the sheet up to her chin. Nechaev angrily confronts the others. The Major relights the candle by the bed.*) What is the meaning of this?

MAJOR

We're from the Third Division. We're looking for a Nickolay Uburnov.

NECHAEV

Well — ?

MAJOR

(*puzzled*) You're Uburnov?

VERA

(*quickly*) And I am Mrs. Uburnov. What do you want?

MAJOR

You're not the man I'm looking for. (*suspicious, unwilling to admit a mistake*) Has anyone else been here?

NECHAEV

Do you think we make love before witnesses? Get out and leave us alone.

MAJOR

(*after a pause*) We apologize for our intrusion. There has been a mistake. (*to the others*) Outside — quickly. (*The Major and policemen leave the room to gather in the street below and pantomime talk. Nechaev sits on the edge of the bed for a moment, thinking, then crosses to the window. Vera sits wide-eyed and shaking in the bed. As Nechaev watches, the Major sends the two policemen off in different directions to search. The Major leans against a nearby building to watch the room and smoke his pipe. Nechaev and he eye each other, then Nechaev turns to Vera.*)

NECHAEV

They are still in the street. They're not quite convinced. Come here.

VERA

To the window? Like this?

NECHAEV

(*nodding*) It will help them believe. (*Somewhat frightened and shy, she wraps the sheet around her, climbs out of bed, and crosses to him.*) Make it look real. Respond. (*He kisses her passionately, caressing her. Slowly, he pulls the sheet from around her. Vera returns his embrace. The Major puffs thoughtfully on his pipe. The loveplay continues, and Vera appears to be caught up in Nechaev's passion; he leads her to the bed, and they kiss once more.*)

131

Finally, he reaches down and extinguishes the candle, plunging the apartment into darkness. They fall upon the shadowed bed, struggling.)

VERA

(*pleading*) Please. They cannot see now.

NECHAEV

That was for them. This is for me.

VERA

(*a cry*) Nechaev . . ! (*The Major seems to hear the cry which echoes around the building. He stands thinking as the policemen run up to him with their lanterns.*)

FIRST POLICEMAN

There's no sign of anyone in the streets.

MAJOR

He may have gone across the rooftops. By now, he and his Moscow friend have escaped us.

SECOND POLICEMAN

(*cynically*) Are you sure you had the right address?

MAJOR

(*a look*) I wasn't, a moment ago, but I've just viewed a most interesting performance — by a man who says he doesn't like witnesses.

FIRST POLICEMAN

Sir — ? (*The Major takes out his notebook and quickly writes a note under the light of their lanterns.*)

MAJOR

(*writing*) I want you to take this note to my headquarters. Have them search the file on "Uburnov." And also see if there is anything under the name "Petrovich." Bring what they find to me at once.

FIRST POLICEMAN

Yes, sir. (*He salutes and hurries off. The Major turns to the second policeman.*)

MAJOR

You wait in that doorway up the block. I may yet need you tonight. (*The policeman salutes and exits. The Major relights his pipe. Above, in the darkness, Nechaev's flute plays a bright, triumphant tune — one which he will play after each of his "victories." After a moment, Vera lights the candle to show herself in a robe by the table. Nechaev lies on his back in bed, playing, as she stands staring into space, then closes her eyes, and takes a deep breath as if breathing fresh air for the first time. Nechaev notices and stops playing to chuckle at her reaction.*)

NECHAEV

Well? Is the new "Uburnov" better than the old?

THE NIHILIST

VERA

(*smiling*) There is no comparison. (*Nechaev laughs and lies back contentedly.*)

NECHAEV

Ah, it's pleasant to lie here with my ass in Hertzen's face. (*He pulls out Hertzen's poster and looks at it.*) Have you read his magazine *The Bell*?

VERA

No.

NECHAEV

I have. (*He throws the poster aside in disgust.*) Drivel. Pap and nonsense. (*He takes out the poster of Bakunin and looks at it. As he talks, Vera cuts the loaf of bread on the table, and pours wine for them.*) Bakunin is another matter. He knows what revolution means. Someday I'll go see him. We could do great work together.

VERA

He's in Geneva, thousands of miles away.

NECHAEV

It won't matter — not if I make up my mind to do it. (*He lays the poster aside and pulls on his trousers and boots.*)

VERA

Is it true that you taught yourself to read and write?

NECHAEV

Of course. Ten years ago. Now I devour every book I can lay hands on — Shakespeare, Dickens, Hugo, Byron, Turgenev, Machiavelli. I drive Kuznetsov wild at the bookstore. I steal his employer's books. (*He laughs.*)

VERA

For a teacher of religion, you're a wicked man.

NECHAEV

Romans 5:20 — "Let us sin more abundantly so that grace may abound."

VERA

(*laughing*) I don't know my catechism that well.

NECHAEV

Let me tutor you. We'll start with the Song of Solomon. (*He crosses to stand behind her at the table, kissing and caressing her in keeping with his words.*) "Kiss me with the kisses of your mouth, for your love is better than wine. Your lips, my bride, are like the honeycomb; honey and milk are under your tongue. Your eyes are as doves. Your neck is a tower of ivory. Your two breasts are like twin fawns which feed among the lilies. The joints of your thighs are like jewels, the work of a cunning workman." (*Feeling herself falling under his spell, she twists away to put the table between them.*)

133

VERA

Even the devil can quote Scripture. (*Laughing, Nechaev picks up his wine and drinks. Recovering, Vera turns to regard him soberly.*) Sergei, why did you become a revolutionary?

NECHAEV

(*with bread in his hand*) Hunger. I'm a very hungry man.

VERA

How much can one man devour?

NECHAEV

(*still playing*) That depends on his appetite. "Teeth had I in my head when I wast born, To signify I came to bite the world." That's from Shakespeare.

VERA

(*still probing*) Why did you join our group?

NECHAEV

Maybe I liked the menu. (*He laughs and she grows angry.*)

VERA

Can't you be serious for a moment? Must you always play the clown?

NECHAEV

(*an abrupt, cold switch*) I play what I want. You'd like me to say I joined because of you. You want to be courted with sweet words and passionate phrases. (*throws the bread on the floor*) I won't do it. There's no time for courtship among revolutionaries.

VERA

And love — ?

NECHAEV

(*points to the bread*) Like food — a thing to be devoured. (*smiling, another mood change*) Even under the eyes of the police. (*Reminded, Vera looks out the window as the first policeman returns with a folder. He gives it to the Major, who studies it under the man's lantern. Above, Vera turns slowly to face Nechaev.*)

VERA

They're still watching. (*a smile*) We haven't convinced them yet. (*Nechaev laughs and crosses to kiss her; she returns his kiss hungrily, and he scoops her up to carry her to the bed. As he lies down with her upon it, Tkachev climbs through the window and stops — stunned at the sight.*)

TKACHEV

Vera! (*Vera springs up guiltily. Nechaev roars at this hilarious situation, then crosses to his glass of wine to drink. Vera crosses to Tkachev.*)

VERA

I'm glad you're safe.

TKACHEV

(*coldly*) Are you? What is the meaning of this?

NECHAEV

If you don't know, your noble father failed his parental obligations.

TKACHEV

(*to Vera*) I came back because I was afraid for you.

VERA

The police?

TKACHEV

And this swine! (*indicates Nechaev*)

NECHAEV

That's not very nice of you, Tkachev. To say your wife sleeps with pigs.

TKACHEV

Get out!

VERA

Niki, please . .

NECHAEV

Afraid of horns, Tkachev? But you're not really married. They're horns "in name only."

VERA

Sergei!

TKACHEV

"Sergei" is it now?

NECHAEV

You're a eunuch, Tkachev. All brains and no balls. You're not man enough for a woman like Vera. It takes more than rhetoric to satisfy her.

TKACHEV

Animal — ! (*He starts for Nechaev, who eagerly grabs the bread knife. Vera throws her arms around Tkachev and pulls him back.*)

VERA

No, Niki. Don't let him provoke you. (*Tkachev subsides, and Vera turns to Nechaev.*) Sergei, I want you to leave.

NECHAEV

Do you prefer the old Uburnov to the new?

VERA

It's not a matter of men. It's a matter of the Revolution. I love it more than either of you. And that means I don't want you to kill each other.(*Nechaev laughs and drops the bread knife on the table. Leisurely he dons his shirt and jacket.*)

NECHAEV

This is a rare woman, Tkachev. She has both mind and spirit. She'll outlast us both.

TKACHEV

She's my wife.

NECHAEV

Didn't you listen? She belongs to the Revolution. Now it remains to see which of us is really the Revolution. (*He crosses and suddenly kisses Vera passionately. To Vera*) He may claim your mind — and respect — but you and I know who claims the rest. Goodnight, comrades. (*He picks up his flute, blows a trill, laughs, and exits. Vera, recovering, runs after him — too late.*)

VERA

Sergei! Not that way! The police! (*She blows out the candle and hurries to the window as the room fades into darkness. Below, Nechaev emerges and walks along the street, playing little trills on his flute. Suddenly, the Major and two policemen block his path and surround him, unshuttering their lanterns. Nechaev stands uncertainly, half-blinded in their light.*)

MAJOR

Sergei Nechaev.

NECHAEV

Pardon? That's not my name.

MAJOR

I know you now. You call yourself by other names, but your real name is Nechaev. (*indicates the folder*) You were born near Vladimir. Your father was a serf, a carpenter. You're licensed to tutor in religion and attend classes at the University. You've also attended radical political meetings.

NECHAEV

(*sounding afraid*) Mrs. Uburnov goes to them. I go to be near her.

MAJOR

You lied to me up there.

NECHAEV

No man tells the truth in a situation like that. And I didn't say I was Uburnov.

MAJOR

You didn't deny it.

NECHAEV

Not in bed with his wife!

MAJOR

Why do you use the name "Petrovich"?

NECHAEV

So Uburnov won't know my real name.

MAJOR

(*with contempt*) And track you down when he learns about your affair with his wife. Where was he tonight?

NECHAEV

Gone.

MAJOR

Obviously. Where?

NECHAEV

I don't know. To a meeting, I think.

MAJOR

Political?

NECHAEV

I don't know.

MAJOR

(*taking his arm*) Come along with us. (*The first policeman takes the other arm, and they begin to pull him along. He resists.*)

NECHAEV

Wait! I'll tell you what I know.

MAJOR

That's better. Where is Uburnov?

NECHAEV

He went to a political meeting. He's always going to them. That's why his wife gets so lonely.

MAJOR

Where is this meeting? When will he be back?

NECHAEV

(*shrugs*) I don't know. Tomorrow sometime. All that matters to me is I left before he got home.

MAJOR

Uburnov must be quite a fool.

NECHAEV

All these idiots are. Holding meetings, screaming about causes. I've got more important things to do.

MAJOR

So I've observed. Who is Ivanov?

NECHAEV

(*shrugs*) I don't know. Some firebrand from Moscow. The damn fool brought the police down on us with his speech today. I nearly got my head cracked.

MAJOR

And you will get it cracked — if you go to any more demonstrations like that. Your private life is your own business, but if I see you again at a demonstration, you'll spend some time in jail.

NECHAEV

(*tugging forelock*) Don't worry, sir. Not even Mrs. Uburnov is worth that risk. You won't see me again, sir. (*The Major considers him for a moment, half in suspicion, half in contempt, not sure he should be released. Then he sighs and turns to the policemen.*)

MAJOR

Let him go. We've wasted enough time with him. (*Nechaev moves quickly and timidly away — but does not exit. He stands watching from across the stage.*) You two can go back to your barracks.

SECOND POLICEMAN

(*needling*) What shall we tell General Trepov?

MAJOR

(*acidly*) Try the truth. Tell him I failed. It will make his whole evening. And one more thing — tell him my failure will be reported — by me. (*He turns and exits. The two policemen look at each other in reaction to this outburst, then exit. A spotlight hits Nechaev, and his manner changes. He shouts after the Major.*)

NECHAEV

Yes, fool, you failed. And you did much worse. You warned me that I was in danger — that you had a file on me. Someday soon, you'll regret that warning. (*He moves to begin his change for the next scene, talking to the audience.*) It's time I was making a name for myself. And now, there's only one place to do that. (*He makes an imperious gesture.*) Geneva! (*He steps out of the light and disappears. The light blinks out.*)

Scene 2

Bakunin's apartment. Cyclorama: slide — the word "Geneva" which fades quickly. Mikhail Bakunin and Nickolay Ogarev enter. The former is fifty-five, graying and paunchy, with a beard and moustache. He is a firebrand, full of nervous energy. Ogarev is tall, thin, late middle-aged, approaching senility — a disenchanted poet and discredited revolutionary. The apartment is modestly furnished, European, and has a couch, bookcase, and writing table covered with materials.

BAKUNIN

Wait till you meet him, Ogarev. He's a man on fire.

OGAREV

I hope he's worth the money I have invested in him.

THE NIHILIST

BAKUNIN

Is money all you can think of?

OGAREV

If I don't think about it, what little I have flies away. Look at you. You're practically penniless.

BAKUNIN

I have no time to think of money. There is too much to be done.

OGAREV

(*wearily*) Do you still intend to fight Marx for control of the International?

BAKUNIN

I'm going to force a decision at the Fourth Congress.

OGAREV

Well, Marx doesn't seem to be very worried. And *he* has time to think of money. For all his hatred of capitalism, he plays the London stock market.

BAKUNIN

He's a hypocrite. I live what I believe in.

OGAREV

And you take in every stray dog or cat who claims to be a Russian revolutionary.

BAKUNIN

Nechaev is different. He came from Russia to help us.

OGAREV

If that's true, he *is* different. Most of your recruits come to help themselves.

BAKUNIN

Nechaev is a true revolutionary. And he has an organization in St. Petersburg to support him.

OGAREV

Good. It will save us the trouble. (*Ogarev picks up some papers on the table and squints at them.*) What are these? Are you still translating French novels?

BAKUNIN

That's the Communist Manifesto.

OGAREV

But Marx and Engels are your enemies.

BAKUNIN

The publisher isn't, and he's the one who's paying me to translate it. I cannot go on borrowing from you. I must take what work I can. Even this trash.

OGAREV

(*sighing*) Be glad you can find work. No one wants Russian poetry. (*Nechaev enters. He is dressed in a modest but fashionable suit of the period. His*

139

hair is combed, and he appears less wild and unruly, more like a clerk in a small bank than a revolutionary.)

BAKUNIN

Nechaev. Come meet my friend Nickolay Ogarev. Nickolay, this is Sergei Nechaev — my latest recruit from our fatherland.

NECHAEV

I am honored to meet such a famous poet and revolutionary. (*He shakes hands and bows stiffly.*)

OGAREV

(*fingering his suit*) You have good taste. How much did this cost me?

BAKUNIN

Nickolay! This man is our guest.

OGAREV

He also hopes to work with us. I want to be sure we can afford him.

NECHAEV

I assure you, I'll earn my keep.

OGAREV

What are your philosophies?

NECHAEV

I believe in the Revolution.

OGAREV

What revolution? There are different kinds.

NECHAEV

The glorious uprising of the People. The one which you yourself so grandly pioneered.

OGAREV

(*pleased*) Pioneer. No one has called me that in a long time.

BAKUNIN

There is no need to question his beliefs. I have done that thoroughly.

OGAREV

And he agrees with you?

BAKUNIN

To the letter.

OGAREV

Then the others may not welcome him. Some fear your constant talk of violence. Do you advocate violence, Nechaev?

NECHAEV

I advocate the uniting of the People and the expression of their will.

OGAREV

That's good . . good. But what of violence?

THE NIHILIST

NECHAEV

I detest bloodshed. The State should yield to the People's will.

OGAREV

Yes — but what of violence?

NECHAEV

Do you believe violence necessary to achieve the People's will?

OGAREV

Of course. It's inevitable in this day of reaction.

NECHAEV

Then don't you also advocate violence?

OGAREV

No!

NECHAEV

But if you believe it inevitable, what does it matter who begins it — the government or the People?

OGAREV

(*confused*) Please, please. You addle me. I'll let Hertzen do the questioning.

BAKUNIN

You invited Hertzen here, knowing how we detest each other?

OGAREV

I'm only thinking of your own good. You're short of money, and the Revolutionary Fund is the best answer.

NECHAEV

(*very interested*) What's that?

OGAREV

A disgruntled nobleman gave Hertzen and me part of his fortune to use for revolutionary purposes in Russia.

BAKUNIN

And they, being good little capitalists, put the money in the bank instead of using it.

OGAREV

(*to Nechaev*) We do use it. In the bank it draws interest. So far, we've been able to print leaflets and help refugees such as yourself by using only the interest.

NECHAEV

And the original money is still intact.

OGAREV

Exactly. Our "capitalism," as Mikhail calls it, is actually most wise.

BAKUNIN

Horse apples! Leaflets of poetry and refugee relief are not "revolutionary

141

purposes in Russia." Give me the money, and I will see that it is put to good use.

OGAREV

I'm willing to give you the money. You know that. But Hertzen won't agree to it. Not until he's convinced you won't use it to start a war. (*There is a knock at the door, and Ogarev starts for it.*) Now you be polite to him, Mikhail. He's very unwell.

BAKUNIN

I'll be polite . . (*an aside to Nechaev*) to his money. (*Ogarev ushers Alexander Hertzen and Natalie into the room. Hertzen is in his late fifties, very gray, with a bald spot. He has a beard and moustache and wears pince-nez glasses. He leans heavily on a cane and appears very ill. His clothes, speech, and bearing reflect his cultured background. Natalie, looking very pale, slowly follows them across the room. She wears drab clothing and has her hair tied back in a harsh fashion.*)

HERTZEN

(*a stiff little bow*) Good day, Bakunin. Has Marx expelled you from the International yet?

NATALIE

Father . . !

OGAREV

(*as Bakunin bristles*) Please. Please. We did not come to talk about the International. Alexander Hertzen, this is Sergei Nechaev. (*Hertzen and Nechaev regard each other carefully. Nechaev puts out his hand to shake, but Hertzen merely nods a bow. Somewhat stung, Nechaev turns toward Natalie.*)

NECHAEV

And who is this attractive young lady?

HERTZEN

My daughter Natalie. Don't try to charm her, Nechaev. She knows how plain she is. (*Natalie reacts unfavorably to this and turns away. Nechaev is quick to notice. He goes to her, takes her hand, and kisses it.*)

NECHAEV

Your father does you an injustice.

HERTZEN

Balderdash! (*to Bakunin*) If that is all the sense your new disciple has, I'm wasting my time here.

BAKUNIN

You came with your mind already made up. You're sour on the younger generation because they reject your out-of-date ideas.

HERTZEN

That's not true.

OGAREV

(*interceding*) Then why not give Nechaev a chance to talk to you? It cannot do any harm.

HERTZEN

Very well, Nickolay. (*pointedly*) For you.

BAKUNIN

(*suddenly*) Before you begin, I wish to make a presentation. Nechaev, please come here. (*Nechaev crosses to him, and Bakunin picks up a piece of parchment from the table.*) Sergei Nechaev, because of your loyalty and dedication to the cause of freedom and equality for all men everywhere, I wish to confer upon you the following honor. This document states: "The bearer of this is one of the accredited representatives of the Russian Section of the World Revolutionary Association, Number 2771."

NECHAEV

(*taking it*) I am honored.

BAKUNIN

This grants you all the privileges of a member in the Committee General of the European Revolutionary Alliance.

HERTZEN

I've never heard of it.

BAKUNIN

It's a secret organization.

HERTZEN

Very secret, I imagine. You two are probably the only members.

BAKUNIN

You would hear more, Alexander Hertzen, if you weren't such a damned snob.

HERTZEN

I hear all I need to *about* you — and more than I care for, *from* you.

OGAREV

Gentlemen, gentlemen, please. Can't we move on to a discussion of the Revolutionary Fund?

BAKUNIN

I won't be insulted by this pig's ass.

HERTZEN

(*starting off*) Come, Natalie. We've wasted our time. Bakunin hasn't changed. Once a jackal, always a jackal. (*Nechaev moves quickly to intercept them.*)

NECHAEV

Comrade Hertzen, if you won't give the money to Bakunin, give it to me. My Russian agents and I will use it to achieve its purpose.

HERTZEN

How? What kind of an organization have you?

NECHAEV

A large one. (*shows him a list*) Here is a list of my members. I've been mailing each of them pamphlets and propaganda to use.

HERTZEN

That must cost a considerable sum.

NECHAEV

Which is why I need your help.

HERTZEN

How would you use the money?

NECHAEV

To purchase a press in Russia, so that I could print our materials there. Then there are passports, travel permits, informers inside the government, weapons . .

HERTZEN

(*quickly*) Weapons?

NECHAEV

To defend ourselves. I'm no cutthroat. I want to carry your message to the People. The message of Revolution.

IIERTZEN

My message is one of reform. I don't want Russia torn apart by a revolution. I want orderly change.

NECHAEV

That is my goal, too. But I need your help. You ideas and leadership are necessary for my success. Won't you help me? I would willingly accept your advice and directions.

HERTZEN

You are Bakunin's protégé. Why would you accept my guidance?

NECHAEV

You are a member of the intelligentsia. You're a wise and temperate man. I'm young and a little impatient, I'm afraid. You could help me overcome that.

HERTZEN

Which Bakunin never could. (*to Ogarev*) Nicholas, I would like to speak to you alone. (*They go off to one side or into a bedroom offstage. Bakunin moves away bitterly from Nechaev, who turns his attention once more to a nervous Natalie. He looks at her for a long time — until she begins to squirm under his gaze.*)

NECHAEV

Are you married?

NATALIE

Me — ? No.

NECHAEV

Do you have a suitor? (*She shakes her head.*) The men of Geneva are fools. May I call upon you tomorrow? (*She looks frantically around for her father, but Hertzen cannot help her. Nechaev takes her hand again, and this time kisses it slowly, holding it until she withdraws it in flustered confusion.*) I shall call for afternoon tea. (*Ogarev and Hertzen return to Nechaev.*)

OGAREV

(*bubbling over*) Comrade Nechaev, we have decided to give you part of the Fund.

HERTZEN

(*sternly*) A probationary grant. To test what you can do with it.

NECHAEV

(*stung somewhat but hiding it*) I will do my best. What are your instructions?

HERTZEN

I'll give them to you tomorrow. You must call on me at my home.

NATALIE

(*quickly*) For tea.

NECHAEV

(*smiling*) I'll be there. It will be an honor to work with you.

HERTZEN

Good. Nicholas and I will go by the bank to withdraw your money. Bakunin, you could take some lessons in manners from your protégé. (*He leads Ogarev and Natalie out, as Nechaev bows. Natalie looks back at him all the way out. Once they are gone, Bakunin strides angrily to the table, takes up a manuscript and rips it in two, flinging the pieces at Nechaev.*)

BAKUNIN

There! Wipe your brown mouth with that!

NECHAEV

(*examining the pieces*) This is our pamphlet.

BAKUNIN

Yes. Our great collaboration — ''the Revolutionary Catechism.'' The secret manual of arms for revolutionaries. Well, you won't be needing it now. You're one of Hertzen's ''reformers.''

145

NECHAEV

(*smiling*) You should have reread it instead of tearing it up. Here . . see what it says about working with your enemies and using them. (*He holds out the pieces, chuckling, and Bakunin begins to understand*.)

BAKUNIN

It was an act?

NECHAEV

My best performance yet.

BAKUNIN

(*laughing*) It was so good even I was taken in.

NECHAEV

(*laughing*) You had to be to make it work.

BAKUNIN

And now we can use Hertzen's money as we please. (*Laughing, he begins to pace*.) First, we'll need a press. That goddamned Marx won't let me use the one that belongs to the International.

NECHAEV

(*sobering*) No. We want all of the Fund — not part. To be sure we get it, we must play Hertzen's game awhile. The money goes back to Russia with me. I can use it there as I see fit, and Hertzen won't be able to check up on me.

BAKUNIN

(*coldly*) What about me?

NECHAEV

I'll see you get enough to live on. (*indicates the papers*) These damned French novels take up too much of your time. You should spend less energy on them and fighting Marx, and more on fighting the Czar.

BAKUNIN

And you're keeping the major portion for yourself — going back with money and a reputation I helped you win.

NECHAEV

Mikhail, the Revolutionary Catechism was my idea. And I persuaded Hertzen.

BAKUNIN

And if you get the rest of the Fund, what then?

NECHAEV

Why then, my friend, perhaps we'll start your war. (*He begins to laugh, and Bakunin finally smiles with him, but he is wary of his protégé now. The lights dim. Nechaev steps into a spot*.) First, an intermission. Then, the triumphal Entry into Jerusalem! (*He signals, and the light blinks out*.)

ACT TWO

Scene 1

The room at the bookstore. Cyclorama: slide — a bloodstained hand upon the Revolutionary Catechism. Fades out. Nechaev's flute plays for a moment. The lights come up on a plain room with a couch, a table, some chairs — spartan living quarters at the bookstore. Vera paces about, nervously smoothing out her new dress. Tkachev watches her with mild amusement. Prizhov lounges on one end of the couch, reading a copy of the Catechism, while Ivanov sits on the other end, impatiently drumming his fingers. Kuznetsov sits primly in a chair. Wine and glasses are on the table. Finally, Ivanov can bear it no longer and stands up, addressing Vera.

IVANOV

Well, where is he? We've been waiting for your hero over an hour.

VERA

He'll be here.

PRIZHOV

Soon, I hope. I'm developing a great thirst.

KUZNETSOV

You've always had a great thirst.

PRIZHOV

(*laughing*) From birth. As a baby, I pulled so hard on my mother I stretched her dugs clear down to here. (*He indicates his waist and roars at his joke.*)

TKACHEV

(*angrily*) Prizhov!

PRIZHOV

(*subsiding*) I'm sorry, Vera.

VERA

(*trying not to smile*) You're forgiven.

IVANOV

Well, Nechaev isn't. What does he think we are — his servants? Just because he knows Bakunin doesn't entitle him to give us orders and keep us waiting.

TKACHEV

(*dryly*) Nechaev is an important man now.

IVANOV

So he keeps telling everyone in all those letters he writes.

KUZNETSOV

Don't forget all those packages he sends.

IVANOV

(*crossing to a pile of material on the table*) Yes, his magnificent pamphlets and propaganda. I'm drowning in the flood of it.

KUZNETSOV

He takes too many chances. The censors will intercept it and trace it to us.

PRIZHOV

This Revolutionary Catechism is good. It says what has to be said.

IVANOV

Bakunin probably wrote it.

VERA

(*stung*) Nechaev's name is on it, too. And don't forget that Ogarev dedicated that poem to him.

KUZNETSOV

Then why has he taken so many weeks to return to St. Petersburg?

IVANOV

(*nastily*) Haven't you heard? He's recruiting for his glorious army of the Revolution.

VERA

We were supposed to be doing the same.

TKACHEV

It's too dangerous.

IVANOV

(*seizing the Catechism from Prizhov*) Because of this. Mailing that damned hogwash has put us all under suspicion. (*He wads it up and throws it under the table. Outside, Nechaev appears with Drovnik, a young man with something of the country bumpkin about him. Both are moustachioed and wear police uniforms. Nechaev gestures to Drovnik about going inside, then dons a false beard. Drovnik pulls a pistol from his holster, Nechaev nods, and they burst in.*)

NECHAEV

(*in false, heavy voice*) Nobody move! This is a police raid! (*The conspirators, save for Kuznetsov, freeze where they are. Kuznetsov screams and tries to run by Nechaev, who grabs him, swings him around, and throws him to the floor where he lies whimpering as Nechaev struts around the room.*)

VERA

(*defiantly*) We have done nothing. Why do you come here?

NECHAEV

(*heavy voice*) I'm led to believe you have some most interesting material here. A Revolutionary Catechism, do you call it? (*Ivanov looks around as if to say "I told you so."*)

148

THE NIHILIST

VERA

(*with a glance at the table*) I don't know what you're talking about.

NECHAEV

(*heavy voice*) It was written by two dangerous revolutionaries — Bakunin and Nechaev. (*spits*)

VERA

(*angry*) How dare you spit — !

NECHAEV

(*heavy voice*) So you know him, huh? Perhaps you're even his lover. Let's see what kind of a woman you are. Kiss me. (*He grabs her and attempts to kiss her. She resists — and in the struggle, pulls off his beard. Surprised momentarily, she looks at it, and Nechaev manages to kiss her. She again resists, then recognizing Nechaev, returns the kiss. The others are aghast.*)

TKACHEV

Vera!

IVANOV

Traitress! (*The two part, laughing. As Nechaev looks around, the others now recognize him. Kuznetsov quickly scrambles up off the floor.*)

TKACHEV

Nechaev!

NECHAEV

(*to Vera, heavy voice*) I can see why that son of a dog is mad about you.

VERA

(*laughing, waving the beard*) Speaking of dogs, I think you lost your tail. (*Everyone but Ivanov and Kuznetsov laughs.*)

NECHAEV

Comrades, meet Andrei Drovnik — a member of the Central Committee. (*Drovnik comes forward, holstering his pistol, and greets each one who is introduced. Nechaev playfully introduces.*) Tkachev, our thinker. Prizhov, our drinker. Kuznetsov, our stinker. Ivanov, who hates me. Vera, who loves me. Where is Sofia?

VERA

She'll be along presently.

DROVNIK

I hear someone coming now.

NECHAEV

Beside the door — quickly! (*Drovnik hides beside the door. Nechaev dons the beard, draws his pistol from his holster, and gestures for the others to raise their hands. Sofia enters, sees the scene, and turns to flee. Drovnik springs from behind and grabs her.*)

149

DROVNIK

You're under arrest!

SOFIA

No! (*She stamps on his foot, and he howls, reaching for it. As he does, she slams an elbow back into his mid-section, doubling him over. She then turns and shoves him backward over some boxes. The others roar with laughter at Drovnik's plight — and Sofia stops, puzzled.*)

NECHAEV

What's the matter, Drovnik? Can't you handle a mere girl?

DROVNIK

(*on the floor*) Mere girl — !

PRIZHOV

Sofia is quite a handful.

DROVNIK

In more ways than one. (*He gets up slowly, rubbing his bruises.*)

SOFIA

What's going on here?

NECHAEV

(*removing his beard*) Nechaev has returned! (*She runs to hug him, and he laughs, holstering the pistol.*) That policeman you so badly mistreated is Drovnik of the Alliance Central Committee. You'd better apologize to him.

SOFIA

(*going to Drovnik*) I am most sorry.

DROVNIK

So am I. That one so pretty could be so . . so . .

NECHAEV

Vicious? (*laughs*) You have a lot to learn about Sofia. You should enjoy the lessons.

PRIZHOV

(*going to the wine*) Are we going to stand around jabbering all night? The guest of honor has arrived. Let's celebrate. (*He pours himself a drink, and the others crowd around to pour drinks and talk.*)

NECHAEV

(*to Vera*) You have a new dress. It's very attractive.

VERA

Thank you. I bought it especially for this occasion.

NECHAEV

And this is an occasion. Comrades, we are now part of a worldwide revolution against tyranny.

IVANOV

How?

THE NIHILIST

NECHAEV

Through the help of Bakunin, Ogarev, and Hertzen, I have linked us to their revolutionary organization. (*waving a paper*) I'm Delegate Number 2771.

IVANOV

What's a piece of paper?

KUZNETSOV

You could have written that yourself.

NECHAEV

I bring you more than that. (*drops a bag of coins on the box*) Money to carry on our work. (*Sofia looks at the coins with Prizhov and Tkachev.*)

SOFIA

Look at all this!

NECHAEV

I have five times that much hidden away.

VERA

(*to Ivanov*) And you doubted him!

IVANOV

I doubt him still.

PRIZHOV

You would doubt the Second Coming.

IVANOV

When Nechaev walks on water, I will believe.

NECHAEV

Perhaps you'd rather go back to your own pitiful group in Moscow.

IVANOV

They aren't as pitiful as this one.

NECHAEV

(*clinking coins*) Do you pity us this, too?

PRIZHOV

I wager he'll stay around. Money talks his language.

NECHAEV

Money talks everyone's language. (*looking around*) How many new members have you recruited? (*There is silence. The conspirators hang their heads. Angrily*) No one? What have you been doing?

TKACHEV

The Third Division is everywhere. There's little chance of doing anything.

NECHAEV

Did you pass out the literature I sent you? (*Vera shakes her head.*) Then that's our first task. We must let the world know about "The People's Revenge."

151

KUZNETSOV

(*skeptically*) What's that?

NECHAEV

Our new name. We'll use it on everything we publish. Ivanov, see that your Moscow section hands out its material.

IVANOV

No.

NECHAEV

What — ?

IVANOV

I don't intend to return to Moscow.

NECHAEV

Why not?

IVANOV

I've heard the Third Division is looking for me there. I won't go back until I know it's safe.

NECHAEV

There is a proclamation which you must post in the student dining rooms.

IVANOV

And have them closed? Where will the students eat? Do you want them to go hungry?

NECHAEV

A hungry man is a good ally.

IVANOV

I won't do it.

NECHAEV

The Central Committee has ordered it.

IVANOV

And who are they? Besides you and this protégé?

NECHAEV

They are the wisest and most experienced men in the Revolutionary Alliance. It would not be wise to oppose them.

IVANOV

To oppose *you* is what you mean. You want to be the leader of everything.

NECHAEV

Someone must lead.

IVANOV

Not you. (*to others*) I say we settle it now. Are we to become the puppets of this fraud? I call for a vote.

PRIZHOV

What is the issue?

THE NIHILIST

IVANOV

I offer myself as our leader. Will you support me?

SOFIA

Who else is a candidate? Niki?

TKACHEV

(*shaking his head*) No.

IVANOV

It is Nechaev and me. I call for the vote. Tkachev? (*He records the vote in a little red notebook.*)

TKACHEV

(*a hesitation, then*) I don't want to work under Nechaev. Ivanov.

IVANOV

Kuznetsov.

KUZNETSOV

Ivanov, of course.

IVANOV

Sofia?

SOFIA

(*clinking coins*) I vote for action not talk. Nechaev.

DROVNIK

So do I.

KUZNETSOV

You can't vote. You're not a member of this group.

NECHAEV

He is a member of the Central Committee.

IVANOV

Then, let him vote there.

NECHAEV

I vote for myself. And the count is tied.

IVANOV

And I untie it by my vote. Prizhov?

PRIZHOV

My vote goes with the plebeian. Nechaev.

NECHAEV

Tied again. And that leaves you, Vera, with the deciding vote. Choose well, my love. (*She looks around unhappily — not wanting this — then makes up her mind.*)

VERA

Nechaev.

IVANOV

Fool!

NECHAEV

You had your vote. Now abide by it. I am the elected leader.

IVANOV

I will never take orders from you. If any of the rest of you come to your senses, I will be in the bookstore, waiting. If not, our association is ended. (*He stalks out, and after a moment, Kuznetsov follows. The others are stunned at this break.*)

TKACHEV

What shall we do?

SOFIA

Go after him. Get him to change his mind.

TKACHEV

(*leaving*) I don't think he will.

PRIZHOV

(*to Nechaev*) What now?

NECHAEV

Leave me alone with Drovnik. (*All but Drovnik leave. Nechaev looks stonily at the worried Drovnik.*) You know what this means. We discussed it.

DROVNIK

But that was theoretical, a discussion of the Catechism.

NECHAEV

The Catechism is not theory — but law. Ivanov must be punished. That is the rule of the Central Committee.

DROVNIK

The Central Committee! I don't even know for sure what it is! Why did you say I was a member of it?

NECHAEV

To impress them, you fool. Didn't you see how Sofia looked at you then? Now help me settle this.

DROVNIK

(*uneasily*) I don't know. We should have a meeting to discuss it. Perhaps a trial.

NECHAEV

(*coldly*) I see. I want to talk to Ivanov alone. (*Drovnik nods uncertainly and leaves to get him. Nechaev stands thinking; he looks at his pistol, then his hands. Ivanov enters.*)

IVANOV

(*haughtily*) Well, have you reconsidered . . ?

NECHAEV

(*quietly*) We must work together, Ivan.

THE NIHILIST

IVANOV

Impossible.

NECHAEV

The Revolution is more important than either of us.

IVANOV

Then let me be the leader — and you work for me.

NECHAEV

The Central Committee does not trust your leadership.

IVANOV

Then the Central Committee is stupid.

NECHAEV

They prefer me.

IVANOV

Then they are idiots.

NECHAEV

This is your last chance. Obey me!

IVANOV

I will never obey a serf! (*Nechaev explodes at this, and seizes a startled Ivanov by the throat. They struggle about the room, knocking over furniture, and the others hear the noise and enter — but freeze just inside, not knowing what to do. Kuznetsov starts forward, but is stopped by Prizhov. Ivanov manages to bite Nechaev's thumb and free himself — but he is starved for air and can only stumble and fall, appealing for help to the others. No one moves. He crawls toward them, and they shrink back. Nechaev looks in horror at his bloody hand, then awkwardly fumbles out the pistol and advances behind Ivanov.*)

NECHAEV

In the name of the Central Committee — (*He fires into Ivanov's back, and Ivanov falls face forward — arm still out appealing. Kuznetsov screams, little shrieks that go on and on as he descends into shock. Prizhov slaps him.*)

PRIZHOV

Shut up.

TKACHEV

(*finding his voice*) In the name of God, why — ?

NECHAEV

He would have betrayed us. He put his vanity above the Revolution.

TKACHEV

(*starting forward*) He may only be wounded —

NECHAEV

No! (*waves the gun*) Stay back, all of you. I executed him on behalf of the Central Committee. As it says in the Catechism.

TKACHEV

(*determined*) I'm going to examine him. (*Nechaev suddenly lowers the gun and fires directly at Ivanov again.*)

NECHAEV

There! Now there is no doubt. (*The others regard him in stunned silence.*) Now listen to me, all of you. Revolution is no party with cakes and tea. It means blood. This kind of blood. Understand that. We are all conspirators in his blood now. None of us can inform on the others — or he'll hang for it. There will be one leader — me! I'll take my orders from the Alliance through the Central Committee — and they must be obeyed without question. Do you understand? You obey the orders — or the Committee will order me to use this again. (*He points the gun at them, and they fall back — frightened, nodding — and he begins to calm down.*) Now . . we can't waste time. Someone may have heard the shots. Prizhov, Tkachev, Kuznetsov, you'll help me dispose of the body, We'll put it in the bookstore's cart and take it to the lake.

TKACHEV

I won't help you. This is no part of my revolution. (*For a moment, he and Nechaev glare at each other, then Nechaev smiles.*)

NECHAEV

Very well. Drovnik, keep an eye on him and — (*a sneer*) the *other women*, and clean up this place. The three of us can manage the body. (*to the others*) Pick him up. (*Prizhov and Kuznetsov help him lift the body. Kuznetsov whimpers.*)

KUZNETSOV

The blood. Oh, the blood . .

NECHAEV

Brace yourself, coward. We'll see a lot of it before the Revolution is over. (*to Vera*) Stay here, I want to be with you tonight. (*He gives her a long look, then follows the others out the door with the body. Sofia gets a rag and begins mopping up the blood, fighting her revulsion. Drovnik rights the furniture, then helps her, and she gives him a grateful look. Tkachev crosses to Vera, who stands stunned, and looks sorrowfully at her.*)

VERA

(*finally*) Please don't say it. I know. My vote led to this.

TKACHEV

(*shaking his head*) It would have happened no matter how you voted. But there is still time.

156

VERA

For what?

TKACHEV

For you to escape what must follow. If you bind yourself to Nechaev, you'll be as damned as he is.

VERA

I know.

TKACHEV

What will you do?

VERA

I don't know. (*She stands, not looking at him, on the verge of tears. He shakes his head sadly and leaves. Sofia and Drovnik exit slowly together, comforting each other. The lights dim down around Vera — who is very very alone. Nechaev's flute plays a low, mournful version of his triumph theme briefly — then laughter begins in the darkness near Vera, growing louder and louder — until Nechaev appears beside her — wet with perspiration and exhilarated, his thumb now wrapped with a handkerchief.*)

NECHAEV

Ivan-Three is gone. I determined his fate after all. (*He laughs and strides around the dimly lighted room. Vera watches him silently.*) The Revolution will move smoothly now. There is no question of authority now. (*chuckling*) Do you know what happened? When we put the body in the lake, Kuznetsov went out of his mind. I had to push him in the lake and hold him under water to calm him. I almost held him under too long. (*He laughs, then speaks coolly.*) Perhaps I should've killed him. We might have put the blame for Ivanov's death on him. He's too weak. He'll have to go sooner or later to protect us.

VERA

And who goes after Kuznetsov? Tkachev? Prizhov? Me?

NECHAEV

(*softly*) Anyone who opposes me. (*moving in on her*) Do you oppose me?

VERA

I don't know. I don't like killing.

NECHAEV

There is no choice. Do you think the Czar will hand us his crown for the asking? Do you think he would hesitate to kill us?

VERA

I don't know.

NECHAEV

You *do* know! And so does anyone who has read the Catechism. (*trying to change her mood*) I've been recruiting, did you know that? That's why

157

I took so long to get here. I stopped in Kazan and Moscow and Tula.
Everywhere I went, I won new converts.

VERA

(*acidly*) Like Drovnik?

NECHAEV

(*sobered by this*) Drovnik will do better — later. He has good steel, but
he needs tempering. When the final moment comes, I'll see he's ready.

VERA

What do you really want in the Revolution?

NECHAEV

To destroy the last vestige of monarchy.

VERA

And replace it with what?

NECHAEV

Whatever is necessary.

VERA

We can't live in everlasting rubble. We must have some kind of structure,
some form of order.

NECHAEV

The Central Committee will decide.

VERA

And who are they?

NECHAEV

The wise and all-knowing. And we are their workers. We must be loyal
to them. (*closing on her*) I fear for your loyalty, Verina.

VERA

I can be loyal. But I must know to what.

NECHAEV

Be loyal to me — as I am to the Central Committee. Can you? (*She nods.*)
I wonder. You did not have the training that a serf has.

VERA

(*with growing intensity*) I had a father who made a broken reed of my mother.
Who made us stand in the snow until we were blue with cold and in the
summer sun until we fainted. He wanted us free from all physical weaknesses.
We went to bed when he said and got up at his call. We did not speak
at meals. We could not play with other children nor be tainted with knowledge.
We were his perfect savages and he was our little czar and autocrat. I have
been trained well, Sergei Nechaev. Test me — and see.

NECHAEV

(*moved, he decides to do just that*) Very well, Verina. Come here. (*He
sits on the couch, and she crosses to him.*) Kneel. (*She does.*) I want you

158

to prove your loyalty to me. (*He slowly unwraps the torn and bloody thumb, holding it before her face. She tries to turn away, but he grips her head with his free hand — and pulls her back.*) This is the new Eucharist, and this is your act of communion. Drink of my blood, Verina. Prove your loyalty and your love. (*He holds the thumb just before and above her, and she now stares at it, fascinated, the blood dripping from it onto her cheek.*) This is my blood which was shed for you. Drink. (*He slowly lowers it to her lips, and her mouth opens to accept it. Her eyes close as she wills herself to the act, and as she works her throat to swallow, she loses herself to what is happening. Nechaev leans toward her, stroking her hair, as she moves her head back and forth, lapping the blood with her tongue. Smiling, he pulls her to him in a bloody kiss — and they kiss long and deep, Vera lost, far lost, drinking of his kiss as she did his blood. Nechaev chuckles in the kiss and then embraces her, his hands beginning to move on her body, and pulls her down atop him on the couch. The lights fade out. In the darkness, Nechaev's flute plays a quasi-religious variation of his triumph theme which climaxes, then dwindles away into the distant sound of police whistles.*)

Scene 2

The room at the bookstore. It is later the same night, and the stage is dark. In the distance, a police whistle blows, then another. They continue to blow at intervals as a match flares, and Nechaev lights a candle on the table. He is dressed only in uniform trousers and boots. Vera sits up on the couch, wearing her chemise. Nechaev listens uneasily as the whistles grow louder, then hurriedly dons the rest of his fake police uniform.

VERA

Hurry. They're all around us. I'll try to delay them. (*The door suddenly flies open, and Tkachev rushes in. Nechaev nearly shoots him with his pistol.*)

TKACHEV

The police are coming! They've surrounded the block. (*Nechaev is now dressed and holsters his pistol. Suddenly, he pulls off Tkachev's coat and tugs at his shirt. Tkachev backs away.*) What are you doing?

NECHAEV

Giving them something to look at. (*He pushes Tkachev down on the couch and tugs off his shirt. There is a racket close at hand, and Nechaev blows out the candle and hides behind the couch in the darkness. The door bursts open, and Trepov leads in the Major and four policemen. The latter have lanterns which they flash wildly about the stage until they discover Tkachev*

*and Vera half-dressed on the couch. They close in on them, pinning them
in the glare of the lights. During the questioning which follows, Nechaev
calmly rises up from behind the couch to mingle with the policemen.*)

TREPOV

You are under arrest. Well, well, it is my old acquaintance Peter Tkachev.
Do you remember me from your last visit to the Ravelin? We had quite
a long talk. (*indicates Vera*) And who is this?

MAJOR

She calls herself Mrs. Uburnov.

TREPOV

A name of convenience. Where is the murderer Nechaev?

VERA

Who?

TREPOV

We know all about him and what he's done. Ivanov's body was found floating
in the lake. And in its pocket was this. (*shows the red book*) A book that
led us here. Where is Nechaev?

VERA

I don't know any such man.

TREPOV

We'll see. (*to the policemen*) Bring in Kuznetsov. And search the room.
(*Two of the men go out: one is Nechaev! The others spread out to search
the room. The Major lights the candle, returning light to the stage, then
picks up the crumpled Catechism. He smooths it out, then dons his glasses
to read it and sort through papers on the worktable. The first policeman
returns with a rumpled, bloody-nosed Kuznetsov. Indicating Vera*) Is this
the woman?

KUZNETSOV

(*nodding frantically*) That's Vera Zasner, Nechaev's lover.

TREPOV

So — ! (*to Vera*) Where is he? (*Vera has been looking around the room for
Nechaev and now realizes how he escaped. She begins to laugh.*)

VERA

He's escaped — right under your noses. (*Trepov regards her, frowning,
and turns to the policemen.*)

SECOND POLICEMAN

There's no sign of him. (*Scowling, Trepov crosses to the Major who is
studying the Catechism and some clipped-together sheets of paper.*)

TREPOV

What have you got there?

MAJOR

A manual-of-arms for a terrorist group. (*significantly*) And what appears to be their membership list.

TREPOV

(*looking*) The numbers reach four thousand!

MAJOR

Probably exaggerated. No group with that many members could keep their existence a secret.

TREPOV

(*angrily*) But there is the list. And until now, you knew nothing about them. That oversight will be reported, I promise you.

MAJOR

We have the list. We'll soon have the members.

TREPOV

You mean *I'll* have them. (*indicates the prisoners*) And then I'll force this trash to tell me where Nechaev has gone. I want my hands on him.

VERA

You had him within reach tonight. He won't give you a second chance. (*She laughs.*)

MAJOR

(*indicating the catechism*) The mind who created this will see we get another chance. He won't be able to help himself. As it says in paragraph one: "The revolutionary is a doomed man . . ."

TREPOV

Exactly. We'll find him. (*a hard look at the major*) If the Major has to poke into every corner in Europe. Bring them along. (*He leads the others out. The Major remains a moment, looking at the Catechism, then exits last — still reading. As the lanterns leave the stage, the lights fade out. Nechaev enters a spotlight downstage, pulling on the suitcoat purchased for him by Ogarev. From the pocket he takes a many-faceted, light-reflecting glass ball to perform the following trick.*)

NECHAEV

Misdirection is the magician's greatest trick. You lead the eye to something over here — while doing something else over here. (*With the "other" hand, he produces a "Magician's Bouquet" — a small object which expands into an artificial bouquet of flowers — and with a gesture appears to turn the glass ball into flowers. The trick should be done slowly and with some craft — but if the audience sees through it, that's all right, too, since that is Nechaev's point.*) Show a policeman a half-naked woman, and you can rob a bank right across the street. Trepov stood right next to me, but like the old Russian proverb says: your elbow is near but did you ever try to bite it? (*He demonstrates and laughs. During the speech above, he has crossed to the Bakunin apartment. The lights come up, and he continues right on with his next speech, as if the above had been part of it — and not partly addressed to the audience.*)

Scene 3

Bakunin's apartment. As the lights come up, Nechaev gives Natalie the magician's bouquet and strides about the room, talking — acting very much in charge and putting on a show for Natalie, who sits on the couch with Ogarev. She wears a black dress but appears much more stylish than before, with a touch of makeup, and cannot take her eyes off Nechaev. Bakunin sits in shirtsleeves at his desk, half-listening and making notations in his diary and on other papers. Ogarev restlessly plays with his cane.

NECHAEV

(*continuing*) So I walked right past them in my police uniform. I wonder what Trepov said when he discovered the ''Eagle of Revolution'' had flown?

OGAREV

I wonder what your fledglings said when they learned you had abandoned them in the nest?

NECHAEV

They knew the risks. They're dedicated revolutionaries. The trial is proving that.

NATALIE

The newspapers say Duke Urusov is doing a good job as their defense attorney.

NECHAEV

(*proudly*) He works for me.

BAKUNIN

(*looking up, skeptically*) Russia's leading liberal?

NECHAEV

All of Russia's liberals work for me. Some of them just haven't found out yet.

BAKUNIN

And what are your plans now?

NECHAEV

To carry on the work of Natalie's beloved father. We'll begin by bringing out a new edition of *The Bell.*

OGAREV

On what?

NECHAEV

The Revolutionary Fund. Right, Natalie?

NATALIE

(*not so sure*) I suppose so.

NECHAEV

It will be a living memorial to her father.

OGAREV

And an excellent vehicle for you.

NECHAEV

(*hard, to Ogarev*) You've grown bitter in your senility, comrade. (*softer, for Natalie*) We work together for a better Russia. The four of us shall do great things with *The Bell*. (*Bakunin puts his diary in the drawer, and gets up, gathering some papers which he puts into a folder.*)

BAKUNIN

You two may, but Nickolay and I have other projects.

NECHAEV

(*angrily*) Translating those stupid French novels — !

OGAREV

(*getting up*) A man must eat.

BAKUNIN

And we also face a showdown with Marx. If all goes well at this Congress, we'll take control of the International.

NECHAEV

You would do better to spend your time fighting our real enemy — the Czar.

BAKUNIN

A revolutionary has many enemies. Hunger is one of them.

NECHAEV

Vanity is another. Beware Marx. He fights to kill.

BAKUNIN

(*donning his coat*) We're ready for him. We've been building toward this moment for a long time. (*to Natalie*) And now, we must leave you.

NECHAEV

(*insisting*) I need your help planning the magazine.

BAKUNIN

You've worked me hard enough, Sergei. And this is more important.

OGAREV

Be wary, Natasha. Don't let him work you half to death. (*a look*) You have no idea to what extremes he is willing to go. (*He crosses to join Bakunin.*)

163

NECHAEV

Bakunin, you will regret this decision.

BAKUNIN

Nechaev, while we're gone, try to find some way to cool this revolutionary zeal of yours. You burn too hotly for your own good. (*Bakunin and Ogarev exit.*)

NATALIE

Is he angry with you?

NECHAEV

(*crossing to the desk*) No, worried. He has much at stake in his battle with Marx.

NATALIE

Will he win?

NECHAEV

(*a private joke*) If he's learned his Catechism.

NATALIE

Catechism?

NECHAEV

Lessons in revolutionary zeal. (*opens the desk drawer, lifts out the diary, and looks at it*) When Bakunin returns, I may have some new lessons for him. (*smiles, puts back the diary, and carefully shuts the drawer*) And now, how about a drink to toast our new partnership? (*He gets a decanter of brandy and pours two glasses during the following.*)

NATALIE

Sergei, I'm not sure about your plan. Ogarev is reluctant, too.

NECHAEV

Of course. He's a tired old man. Starting such a project isn't easy for him.

NATALIE

Are you sure it's the best way to spend the money? There are so many other ways that seem better.

NECHAEV

Nothing would be better than carrying on your father's work.

NATALIE

Is it my father's work? Or yours?

NECHAEV

The work of the Revolution.

NATALIE

But what does *that* mean? How do I know your philosophy is the same as my father's? How do I know anything you say is true?

NECHAEV

(*giving her a glass*) Trust me, Natasha.

THE NIHILIST

NATALIE

(*turning away to sit on the couch*) I don't know who to trust anymore. Since Father died, the world's fallen in on me.

NECHAEV

(*sitting beside her*) Then let's not talk of work — or money. Let's see that you're happy first. Your joy before all. (*He clinks his glass against hers, smiles, and she slowly smiles back. As they drink, the lights dim. If feasible — during the following trial scene — they can continue to drink in dim outline, as Nechaev carefully moves in on her.*)

Scene 4

The courtroom. In the darkness, a judge's gavel raps slowly three times. Cyclorama: a slide appears — the Imperial Eagles. It holds until the end of the scene. The lights come up on the courtroom, which consists of a judge's bench, a prisoner's dock, and a table and chairs for the attorneys. Vera, Tkachev, Drovnik, Sofia, Prizhov, and Kuznetsov are in the dock. The Major stands to one side, observing. The Judge is in his late fifties, bearded and gray. He wears a long robe and judicial hat. The Prosecutor is in his late forties, and wears steel-rimmed glasses and a beard. The defense counsel is Duke Urusov, grayer now but still elegant in court clothes, using pince-nez glasses to refer to his notes. Four policemen guard the room, with Trepov very obviously in charge. A policeman stands at either end of the dock, and a new character is present: the Corporal. He is a Ravelin guard in a semi-military uniform with truncheon but no sidearm. He is a stocky young man, likable but not too bright. Like most guards, he's a man who won't be missed elsewhere and is not entirely happy with, or suited to, his job. Everyone is now settled, and the Judge raps again.

JUDGE

Because the prisoners have not denied their guilt, there can be no question of the verdict. Before pronouncing sentence, however, the court will hear arguments for and against leniency. (*one rap*) Duke Urusov for the defense.

DUKE

(*rising*) I choose not to argue on behalf of the accomplices Prizhov and Kuznetsov. I leave their fate to the good judgment of this court. My concern is for the other defendants — these men and women who acted in good faith but were trapped between government obstinacy and Nechaev's duplicity. (*indicates them*) These four did not take part in Ivanov's death.

But they are charged with other "crimes," and it is true they do not deny their "guilt" — for, unlike the prosecution, they do not see them as "crimes."

During this trial, it has been demonstrated by the defense that, in fact, they are not crimes at all — but essentially patriotic acts.

What were these acts? Demonstrations at the University; organizing a secret club to discuss reform; distributing tracts criticizing the government; possessing material banned by a censor infamous for his reactionary attitudes and repression. Are these really "crimes"? No! They are acts of frustration, acts of idealistic endeavor, acts toward long-needed reform.

If they are guilty of anything, it is of wanting a better Russia. Of wanting reform in a backward, decadent nation. And seeking to bring about change.

But one man has tainted their well-meaning goals. One man saw in their naiveté and inexperience an opportunity to aggrandize himself. Sergei Nechaev! He should be on trial here today, not them. It was he who perverted their mission, he who twisted it to his own, evil ends. With lies, deceit, and murder he ensnared them — and then left them to face this court for *his* crimes. *His!* You cannot damn them for his evil. (*at Trepov*) You must find and try *him*.

(*back to the Judge*) The acts of these defendants were committed for our own good. They attacked what is wrong in our society: *our* failures, *our* hypocrisies, *our* evils. Can we punish them for trying to improve us? No! It is we who must change, we who must improve, we who must see that no more of our children are victims of our own shortcomings. If we create a better society ourselves, then our children will not try to do it for us — and in so doing fall prey to the Nechaevs of this world.

The prosecution has labeled these brave men and women radicals, conspirators, revolutionaries, anarchists, nihilists. Every blood-curdling term in the lexicon has been used to arouse anger against them. But I feel no anger toward them. There should be no anger in this courtroom against them. If there is to be anger, it should be anger against a society whose evils led them to rebel. If there is anger, let it be against any man who would want such conditions to continue. If there is anger, let it fall upon any man who would punish these idealists in the name of justice and thus deny us any hope for a better world.

(*to the Judge*) Your honor, you yourself can begin the creation of that better world. Your judgment today can show there is leniency for those who make an occasional mistake in their earnest pursuit of reform. Be truly just. Judge both them and us — and then act for the future good of our country. (*He sits, and after a moment, the Prosecutor rises.*)

PROSECUTOR

My esteemed colleague is a great lawyer. His closing argument today proves that. He has somehow turned the whole trial around. It is not the men and women in the dock who are on trial here. It is the government. It is us. It is Russia herself!

How can that be? Well . . in his idealist way, he seems to argue that unless society itself is perfect, then any crime against it is not a crime but a blow against decadence. These "patriots" did not lie, they did not spread vile propaganda, they did not conspire against their own society, they did not murder . . they were trying to "create a better world."

To carry that argument to its logical conclusion, if your neighbor is short-tempered or long-winded or nearsighted or hunchbacked — he is therefore imperfect, and you are free to murder him and take what he has. Of course, he is free to do the same thing to you — if you are not perfect. But then, you are perfect, are you not? And being perfect, you have nothing to worry about.

This is the better world they would create. A jungle of animals tearing at each other, anarchy, rubble! You have seen a picture of that world in Nechaev's Catechism — their manual of revolution. (*He waves a copy of it.*) No life is worth anything save what it means to the Revolution. People are to be used, blackmailed, killed — as the leaders see fit. The brigand, the robber, the killer are the true revolutionaries because they attack a decadent, materialistic society. It's all there. Read it! This is their *better world*!

But Urusov does not see this as dangerous. He sees it as a promise of brighter tomorrows. He dances with joy on the edge of the abyss!

Our society is not perfect because *we* are not perfect. To destroy the flaws in society means to destroy ourselves. And that is the message these nihilists give us. "Be perfect or we will destroy you without mercy!" They have made themselves the judges of what will be tolerated. And the penalty for those who do not live up to their standards is death!

The defense appeals to your heart. He calls these anarchists our children. Our naive, idealistic children. But they are not children. They are savages. And their acts are not patriotism but treason! Such fanatics, such destroyers, whatever their reasons for rebellion, are still criminals. They must be treated as such. There must be no tyranny of the emotions. There must be cold, hard justice. The law specifies the penalties for their crimes. I call for the strictest application of those penalties. (*Glowering at the prisoners and Urusov, he sits. The Judge gavels, then uneasily consults some papers, obviously stalling as he considers. Then he makes up his mind and gavels again.*)
JUDGE
We find the defendants guilty as charged. The prisoners will rise for sentence.

(*They do.*) Though guilty you are, there are varying degrees of guilt among you. As defense counsel has stated, some of you were obviously well intentioned, but were deceived by Nechaev and his lies. Therefore, this court will deal with you accordingly. (*raps*) We sentence the murder accomplices Prizhov and Kuznetsov to fifteen years in Siberia. (*They react.*) The remaining four are sentenced to six months' confinement, said sentence to have subtracted the time already spent in prison. This court stands adjourned. Remove the prisoners. (*Raps to conclude. The court dissolves. The police herd the prisoners downstage. Sofia and Drovnik stay together, holding hands, and Tkachev walks with a protective arm around Vera. Prizhov and Kuznetsov shuffle along, heads down, until the police stop the prisoners where Trepov, the Major, and the Corporal await them downstage.*)

TREPOV

(*indicates Prizhov and Kuznetsov*) Take those murderers to the train for Siberia. (*As the police try to separate them, the prisoners say hurried farewells, hugging, shaking hands, etc. Prizhov tries to be brave, but is obviously shaken, and Kuznetsov is weeping openly. Two policemen take them away.*) As for the rest of you . . I've been given the authority to make this statement to you. If any of you will tell me where Nechaev is, the Czar will commute your sentence. (*There is no response. Frowning, he crosses to them.*) You might as well tell me. Your revolution is dead. All your comrades are in jail.

SOFIA

Only seventy-nine.

TREPOV

That's all there are.

VERA

There were over four thousand.

MAJOR

You heard the testimony. The numbers were a code. Designed to make the group seem larger.

TREPOV

You're protecting a man who made a fool of you.

MAJOR

Why go to prison for a man like Nechaev?

TKACHEV

We're going to prison because we believe in the Revolution.

SOFIA

The sentence was a slap on the wrist.

DROVNIK

We'll be out in no time.

THE NIHILIST

TREPOV

And do what?

VERA

Begin again.

TREPOV

That would be very foolish. Who will help you now? All your liberal friends have heard how Nechaev used them and ridiculed them.

VERA

Yes, that was a mistake. We trusted too much in Nechaev's methods. But his goals were good.

TKACHEV

You made mistakes, too.

MAJOR

How?

TKACHEV

The trial. You gave us what we never had before — an audience.

SOFIA

You thought you were exposing our conspiracy to the world. Instead, you've exposed the world to our ideas.

VERA

All of Russia knows our goals now — to free the People from misery and oppression.

TREPOV

They also know of Nechaev's deceptions.

DROVNIK

But they blame *him* for them — not us.

TKACHEV

Our motives were good ones, and our goals were the goals of the People. That's what they'll remember.

MAJOR

He has a point.

SOFIA

By trying us, you made everything we worked for easier.

TREPOV

We'll see how easy you think it is after some time in prison. (*to the policemen*) Take them away.

MAJOR

(*indicates Vera*) I'd like her left behind.

TKACHEV

What are you going to do with her?

TREPOV

That no longer concerns you.

TKACHEV

(*struggling with the guard*) Vera — ! (*The policemen take out the prisoners, but the Corporal remains waiting for Vera. As counterpoint to the scene which follows, we might also see simultaneously Nechaev's seduction of Natalie in the Bakunin apartment: kissing, caressing, removing the comb from her hair to let it down around her shoulders, unbuttoning her blouse, and kissing her bare shoulder.*)

TREPOV

(*to the major*) If you don't mind, I'll stay and watch. I'd like to see the famous Third Division in action.

MAJOR

You may find it a little dull, General. No tortures or bloodletting. (*As Trepov glares at him, he signals the Corporal to get a stool.*)

VERA

Then why am I here?

MAJOR

(*offhand*) To chat. (*He gestures for her to sit down, takes out his pipe, fills it, and lights up as they talk.*)

VERA

(*still suspicious*) About what?

MAJOR

How about Tkachev? He's still in love with you, you know.

VERA

(*sitting; sadly*) That's his misfortune.

MAJOR

Are you still in love with him? (*She looks silently at him.*) How about Nechaev?

VERA

(*sharply*) That's none of your business.

TREPOV

That's precisely his business. He's paid to poke and pry.

VERA

It's a dirty business.

TREPOV

Someone has to haul the garbage.

MAJOR

I merely smell it out. (*to Trepov*) You haul it in. (*They exchange sharp looks. To Vera*) The General took all the credit for arresting you nihilists.

THE NIHILIST

TREPOV

Because you didn't even know they existed until we raided the bookstore.

VERA

It's interesting to find you equate nihilists with garbage.

MAJOR

Are you offended?

VERA

Why should I be? I'm no nihilist.

MAJOR

Oh — ?

VERA

I'm a populist, a reform socialist.

TREPOV

Who cohabits with Nechaev, the greatest nihilist of them all.

VERA

He isn't like the others. He isn't all talk.

TREPOV

No, he kills people!

MAJOR

Would you kill for your cause?

VERA

(*she isn't sure*) Yes, I suppose I would — if I had to.

MAJOR

Are you going on with your cause, then?

VERA

Of course. We've only begun.

MAJOR

And will you kill?

VERA

I'm against violence. I want peaceful reform. (*to Trepov*) If people like you will ever allow it.

TREPOV

And if we don't?

VERA

You must be destroyed!

TREPOV

(*stung, moving in*) Is that what Nechaev taught you?

VERA

Yes — and he was right. You're evil and corrupt. You work for the most decadent government that ever existed on the face of the earth. You can't escape its guilt by pretending you're only doing your job. (*In Bakunin's*

171

apartment, Natalie succumbs during the following, and the lights go out there.)

TREPOV

(leaning angrily over her) And Nechaev isn't evil or corrupt? *(She shakes her head.)* After he lied about his exploits, murdered Ivanov, and abandoned you to us?

VERA

(rising to face him, shaken but unbending) I will not deny him! *(For a moment, they confront each other, then Trepov turns to the Corporal.)*

TREPOV

This interview is over. Get this stupid bitch out of here! *(The Major starts to protest, then changes his mind and shrugs. The Corporal, impressed by Vera's defiance of them, respectfully escorts her out. She gives Trepov a look of contempt as she exits, which further infuriates him.)* Damn her! Damn all their women! They're worse than the men. *(sarcasm)* And they breed new revolutionaries. *(The Major has enjoyed Vera's defense, too, and smiles. Trepov notices and turns his sarcasm on him.)* So that's the great Third Division's method of interrogation. Chatting. Well, you didn't find out much from her.

MAJOR

Perhaps. But then I really didn't expect much. Especially with you here.

TREPOV

(bristling) Why not?

MAJOR

First, because of who and what you are. Second, because she still loves Nechaev. Fortunately, there are others who don't. *(He smiles, nods, and exits before Trepov can ask what he means. Trepov is left alone and angry as the lights fade out.)*

Scene 5

Bakunin's apartment. Cyclorama: slide — a small diary or journal. It fades out. The lights come up on an empty apartment. Nechaev's suit coat hangs over the couch, and his flute is heard playing his triumph theme in the bedroom. It stops as Ogarev angrily stomps into the room, a pamphlet in one hand, his cane gesturing violently in the other. Bakunin follows as if in a daze. He, too, carries a pamphlet crushed in his big hands.

OGAREV

Where is he? Damn him! I'll cane him! *(Nechaev appears in the bedroom doorway, buttoning his shirt, a little disturbed by their arrival.)*

NECHAEV

Home so soon, comrades? (*Ogarev crosses to wave the pamphlet under his nose.*)

OGAREV

Now you've done it, you miserable bastard! Now you've done it!

NECHAEV

(*pushing the pamphlet aside*) Done what?

OGAREV

We've been expelled from the International. Because of you. (*Natalie enters from the bedroom in time to hear this speech. Her hair and clothes are slightly mussed, and the top buttons on her blouse are undone. For a moment, they do not notice her.*)

NECHAEV

Me — ?

OGAREV

(*waving the pamphlet*) Marx put out a pamphlet describing your crimes. He turned the whole Congress against us.

NECHAEV

What crimes?

OGAREV

Your operations in Russia. It's all here — robbery, deceit, murder! You deserve a good beating! (*Ogarev raises his cane, but Nechaev suddenly seizes it and twists it away, sending the old man to the floor. Nechaev leans over him, raising the cane.*)

NATALIE

Nechaev, no — ! (*He glares a moment at Ogarev, then throws the cane aside in disgust, and stalks over to the desk. Natalie crosses to help Ogarev to a chair. Bakunin just now realizes what has happened between her and Nechaev, and his sense of outrage at her seduction helps bring him back to reality.*)

BAKUNIN

Nechaev! You and Natalie — ? (*He gestures toward the bedroom.*)

NECHAEV

(*still smoldering*) Of course. Why not? (*Natalie reacts in embarrassment, further angering Bakunin.*)

BAKUNIN

You are despicable.

NECHAEV

Why? Because I made love to Natalie? Or because of those lies Marx tells about me? (*snorts*) The Third Division probably put him up to it.

BAKUNIN

But he expelled *me*!

NECHAEV

Well, you're the one who's been fighting him. What did you expect? He'd do anything to get at you — even use lies about me. (*Ogarev sees Bakunin weakening and waves the pamphlet.*)

OGAREV

Don't listen to him, Mikhail. They're true. Marx documents them all in this. (*Natalie takes the pamphlet from him and begins to read it.*) It's all in there. There is no Russian section. No Central Committee. All lies.

NECHAEV

There was a Russian section — ''The People's Revenge.''

BAKUNIN

With seventy-nine members?

OGAREV

You said *thousands*!

NECHAEV

There would have been — eventually.

BAKUNIN

(*growing furious again*) Seventy-nine!

NECHAEV

(*fighting back*) How many members were in your damned ''World Alliance'' when you made me member 2771? Count, Bakunin. Count and tell us who is the bigger liar about memberships. (*Bakunin backs down a little, but Natalie holds out the pamphlet.*)

NATALIE

It says you tricked my father. You took the Revolutionary Fund and used it for your own purposes.

NECHAEV

My ''purposes'' are the Revolution. The money was spent on propaganda, weapons, and bribes.

OGAREV

That's what *you* say.

NECHAEV

Who in this room has any evidence to the contrary? Have any of you ever seen me spend a penny on myself? See? I wear the same suit you bought me. I eat half what Bakunin does — on money I earn as a sign painter. I don't go to the theatre as you do, Ogarev, and I borrow what books I have. No one can accuse me of misusing the Fund.

BAKUNIN

(*wavering*) But you murdered Ivanov.

174

NECHAEV

I executed him. He was going to betray us.

NATALIE

(*indicates the pamphlet*) This says you killed him because he threatened your leadership.

NECHAEV

Also a perfectly good reason. The successful leader deals ruthlessly with those who oppose him. Like Marx, eh Mikhail?

NATALIE

(*dismayed*) It also says there was a girl. Your lover. Who you left behind to be captured.

NECHAEV

She delayed the police so I could escape. It was her choice.

NATALIE

But she is in jail now because of it, and you told me there was no other woman in your life. Oh, Nechaev, you've made a fool of me, too. (*She sinks down on the couch, holding the pamphlet.*) I never want to see you again.

BAKUNIN

Nor I. Our association is ended. Leave my home.

OGAREV

(*gleefully*) Good! Good!

NECHAEV

Is this the way the noble Bakunin rewards his friends?

BAKUNIN

I took my lessons from you.

OGAREV

(*cackling with glee*) Any more lessons for us now, Nechaev? (*Nechaev angrily spins on his heel and goes into the bedroom. Ogarev howls with laughter. Bakunin crosses to comfort Natalie. Nechaev reappears with a meager handful of clothes and a battered paper suitcase. As he throws the clothes into the suitcase, Ogarev shakes his finger at him. Laughing*) The teacher is out of lessons.

NECHAEV

(*turning*) Not quite. Bakunin, I'm going to London. But you're going to write me a letter of introduction to your friends there.

BAKUNIN

And if I don't — ?

NECHAEV

(*smiling*) Where is your diary? (*Bakunin looks at him for a moment in puzzlement, then begins to comprehend. He races to the desk where he searches fruitlessly through the drawer. Nechaev begins to laugh; Ogarev and Natalie look on, bewildered.)*

BAKUNIN

Gone! Gone! *(to Nechaev)* Where is it?

NECHAEV

Safe. Now write the letter of introduction, Mikhail. And beware how you word it! *(With a roar of frustration, Bakunin seizes pen and paper and rushes off into the bedroom. Ogarev advances on Nechaev, waving his fist.)*

OGAREV

Thief! Thief!

NECHAEV

Precisely. By the way, I have your diary, too — and a packet of very damaging letters. *(Ogarev recoils in horror, then flees after Bakunin as Nechaev roars with laughter. Natalie slowly comes forward, shaking her head, close to panic at these revelations.)*

NATALIE

What kind of man are you?

NECHAEV

A dangerous one.

NATALIE

Do you steal from everyone?

NECHAEV

(nodding) For my own protection. Revolutionaries have a way of turning on each other. Even friends. So I collect things to keep my comrades in line. *(crossing to the desk)* Natasha, to make my new start, I'll need the rest of the Revolutionary Fund. Write out a bank draft for it.

NATALIE

(comprehending in horror) Do you have something of mine, too?

NECHAEV

(smiling) Enough to get what I want. *(He forces her to sit at the desk and pushes a pen into her hand. She looks at him, close to tears, then begins to write. Bakunin enters with Ogarev and throws down a sheet of paper on the desk before Nechaev. He picks it up. Reading)* Very good. Says much without really saying anything. Bakunin, you should have been a bureaucrat. *(Natalie rises and hands Nechaev the bank draft.)*

NATALIE

There! And may God damn you for your sins!

NECHAEV

(smiling) Including fornication — ? Goodbye, Natasha. *(She turns away in self-disgust and torment, almost crying, but too proud to break down in front of Nechaev.)*

BAKUNIN

You're a cruel and vicious man.

NECHAEV

Yes, Mikhail. I believe what we wrote in the Catechism. For me, there is nothing but the Revolution. I'm willing to do anything for it. The man who leads the new Russia will have to. You're not too old to learn that lesson. You made a start on it earlier when you were so ruthless with me. Keep it up and someday you'll be successful. (*laughing*) You can practice on Marx. He's a worthy opponent. In your place, I would have defeated him — because I know how to fight. (*He laughs again and pockets the letter and bank draft.*)

ORAGEV

Someday you'll come down. Someday you'll crawl whining on your belly like the cur you really are.

NECHAEV

(*closing the suitcase*) Old man, I'm tired of your metaphors. It will be good to be free of them. (*locking it*) Why don't you do the world a favor and die?

BAKUNIN

I hope someday I get another chance at you.

NECHAEV

It would be a most interesting encounter. But remember your diary, Mikhail — (*turning hard*) and also remember this. No one can defeat me, because I won't accept defeat. For me, it doesn't exist. I can overcome anything. My spirit conquers all!

NATALIE

Then God help us.

NECHAEV

If He exists. But then, why not? The devil does. Haven't I worked with him myself? (*He laughs and crosses to the door with his suitcase.*) Farewell, comrades. You'll be hearing from me. (*He exits, laughing, and they stand staring after him. The lights fade out on the apartment. Nechaev moves downstage into a spotlight where the Major and a policeman suddenly materialize beside him.*)

MAJOR

(*puffing pipe, genially*) Good day, Nechaev. We've come to the end of the chase.

NECHAEV

(*coolly*) I'm afraid you're mistaken. (*reaches in his pocket*) Here, these papers will identify me as Hans Liders, a sign painter. (*He holds out the papers; the Major nods to the policeman, and he snaps a handcuff over the extended wrist. Quickly, he forces Nechaev to drop the suitcase and locks the other wrist in front, then takes Nechaev's pistol.*)

MAJOR

(*takes the suitcase*) Don't worry about this. I'll carry it for you.

NECHAEV

(*growing angry*) No! It didn't happen this way. This comes later. I went to London. And I was in Paris when we overthrew Louis Napoleon and established the commune.

MAJOR

You played a very small part. It was Bakunin and Ogarev who led the Lyons government.

NECHAEV

Yes, old Bakunin finally learned how to fight. But he told lies about me. He turned the others against me.

MAJOR

So — ? The Lyons government soon fell apart, and Bakunin and Ogarev returned to Geneva to die in exile. What does it matter?

NECHAEV

It matters because it was a promise of things to come. Our Revolution dethroned its first king.

MAJOR

Why fret? That's all past now, and your best moments are just ahead. Nechaev — defiant in chains. Let's get on with your greatest scenes.

NECHAEV

Why not! They'll show who won. Me! The Eagle of Revolution. Not you scum. You're nothing but worms.

MAJOR

(*smiling*) Nechaev, in the end, the worms always win. (*Puffing pleasantly, he indicates for Nechaev and the policeman to move off. As the stage lights adjust, they cross to Nechaev's cell in the Ravelin and leave him standing there glowering as they exit with the suitcase. Nechaev looks at his handcuffs, then turns to the audience.*)

NECHAEV

I should have expected this. No story you tell ever goes quite the way you wanted it. (*relaxing*) But I know the ending, so what does it matter? (*Laughing, he fishes his flute from his pocket and sits down against the wall to play a merry little tune.*)

Scene 6

Nechaev's cell and the courtroom. Cyclorama: slide — Nechaev's flute.
Fades slowly under music. The lights come up on his bare, gray cell in
the Ravelin. Trepov enters with the Corporal, but Nechaev does not stand
up.

TREPOV

I am General Trepov, chief of police. (*Nechaev salutes him with the flute.*)
I've come to offer you leniency in return for a complete confession of your
activities. Should you repudiate what you have done, the government may
take pity on you. Well? (*He waits.*) Well . . ?

NECHAEV

Why don't you go eat a handful of horse dung? (*Trepov swells in rage,*
then controls himself. He sees the flute.)

TREPOV

(*indicating it*) Confiscate that. (*The Corporal takes it and pockets it.*)

NECHAEV

(*very agitated by this*) Why?

TREPOV

Prisoners have no personal property. (*to the Corporal*) Bring him along.
(*Trepov turns and moves out of the cell, with Nechaev and the Corporal*
following. They wait outside and are joined by the Major and two policemen.)

NECHAEV

Well, I am honored to join the parade.

TREPOV

Silence! (*The group marches up to the courtroom, where the lights come*
up to reveal the Judge and Prosecutor waiting. Nechaev is placed in the
dock with a policeman on either side and the Corporal behind.)

JUDGE

(*gaveling*) Order in the court.

NECHAEV

This is no court. It's a farce.

JUDGE

(*gaveling*) Order, order!

NECHAEV

I'm a refugee, kidnapped from another country. I do not recognize this court.
I don't recognize your emperor. I do not answer to your laws.

JUDGE

(*gaveling*) The prisoner will be silent!

NECHAEV

The People will not be silent. You will hear from them.

179

JUDGE

(*gaveling*) Sergei Nechaev, you are accused of plotting the overthrow of your country.

NECHAEV

This isn't my country. I'm a refugee from tyranny. The laws of this country don't concern me. A Russian tyrannist court has no right to try me.

JUDGE

(*gaveling*) Will you be silent, sir!

NECHAEV

You can never silence what I stand for. Freedom for the Russian people. Down with the Czar!

JUDGE

(*furiously gaveling*) Gag the prisoner! Gag him! (*Nechaev struggles with the policemen as they attempt to gag him, escaping momentarily but recaptured with the help of the Corporal. Finally, he is gagged – but his hands are still free. He sits with clenched fists.*) Sergei Nechaev, you are accused of high treason and murder. How do you plead? (*Nechaev gestures to the gag, and the Judge is embarrassed. He signals the policemen to loosen it.*)

NECHAEV

My crimes are political, and I should be tried as a political prisoner — but you choose to try me as a common criminal. You allow me no counsel and you gag my protests. You decide how I plead, fat-ass.

JUDGE

(*furious*) Gag him! (*The gag is replaced.*) The defendant does not deny the charges. Let them be entered into the record as unopposed. (*Nechaev signals for the Judge's attention. The Judge turns to him, and Nechaev pantomimes for him to listen, then "plays the piano" on the dock railing. Finishing, he asks the Judge in sign language how he liked it. The Judge is growing enraged.*) Bind his hands behind him. I will have no more of this foolishness. He shall ridicule this court no further. (*Nechaev's hands are bound, and he appears ready to sit quietly.*)

PROSECUTOR

(*rising*) On the advice of eminent authorities, I've been asked to have the testimony of the government's witnesses entered in the record without reading it in court. It is felt there is no need to inflame the People's anger further with the details of this criminal's villainy. (*During the latter part of this speech, Nechaev has wiggled off one of his shoes and now puts his bare foot up on the dock rail. He wiggles his toes at the Prosecutor. The Judge gavels furiously.*)

THE NIHILIST

JUDGE

Bind his feet! I will have no more of this. (*Nechaev puts up his other foot, and is tied. The Corporal puts on the shoe. To the Prosecutor*) Make your statement.

PROSECUTOR

Sergei Nechaev represents everything which is vile and detestable in man. He is a traitor, a revolutionary, and a murderer. He deserves to be sunk in the lowest pits of hell. (*At these words, Nechaev gives out a gagged shriek and slowly, comically, sinks out of sight behind the railing. The Judge is livid now.*)

JUDGE

(*shouting*) I will not have this! Remove the prisoner! Remove the prisoner! (*The two policemen yank Nechaev to his feet and start him off. He hops merrily along between them.*)

TREPOV

(*roaring*) No, you fools! Drag him! (*They pull him off his feet and drag him outside. Trepov and the Major follow. The lights dim on the courtroom but do not go out. The Prosecutor continues to pantomime his case.*) Remove his gag. (*It is done.*) You idiot! What do you hope to gain by such behavior?

NECHAEV

An audience.

TREPOV

For buffoonery?

NECHAEV

The buffoonery draws the crowd. Then I sell my little patent medicines. Step right up, ladies and gentlemen. Hear how Nechaev would cure the ills of Russia. Buy his revolutionary tonic. Guaranteed to kill tapeworms, hookworms, despots, and czars. Hurry, hurry, hurry. Who will be the first to kill a Romanoff?

TREPOV

(*slapping him*) Silence!

NECHAEV

Even my silence will roar like thunder. You cannot gag the truth. The monarchy is doomed. Revolution is inevitable. You and your kind will go down with it.

TREPOV

You will go down long before.

NECHAEV

True — but you'll go down, too — and that's all that matters. (*In the courtroom, the Judge gavels. The Prosecutor comes out to them.*)

WILLIAM N. MONSON

PROSECUTOR

He's been found guilty. They're ready to pronounce sentence. He must be in court for that.

NECHAEV

But for nothing else.

TREPOV

No platforms in court for you today. (*Nechaev is dragged back into court, somewhat bitter and subdued.*)

JUDGE

(*gaveling*) Sergei Nechaev, you have been found guilty of high treason and murder. I therefore sentence you to the loss of all civic rights, to twenty years' hard labor in the mines, and to forced residence in Siberia so long as you shall live. This court is closed. (*gavels*)

NECHAEV

It is close-minded. Long live freedom! Down with despotism! Down with the Czar! (*The Judge and Prosecutor exit. The others gather around Nechaev, free his legs, and march him out of the courtroom. The Major steps aside and watches as outside the procession is joined by a police drummer, who beats a long roll on his drum. A sign is placed on Nechaev: "For murder!" The group marches about the stage until it reaches a platform with a block upon it. A hooded Executioner waits there with an ax. As the march proceeds, Nechaev shouts over the drum taps.*) Down with the Czar! Free yourselves from your yoke! You are the free Russian people! Remove the Czar from your necks! Down with the Czar! (*People drift onstage to watch, including Duke Urusov and the students we'll know later as Shiraev, Kibalchich, and Ulyanov. Nechaev is marched to the foot of the platform. He sees the Executioner and exults at his coming martyrdom.*) So this is the justice of Russian courts. This is what *exile* really means.

TREPOV

(*to the drummer*) Drown out his vomit! (*The drummer beats loudly, and though Nechaev repeats his shouted message against the Czar, above, he cannot be understood. The policemen place him in position, kneeling at the block. The Executioner raises his ax, the drum stops, and the ax descends. A woman screams in the crowd below, but the ax stops just above Nechaev's neck. He opens his eyes and looks around in bewilderment. The policemen raise him up and take him off the platform.*)

NECHAEV

What is this? What's happening?

TREPOV

The execution is symbolic. It signifies the death of your citizenship.

NECHAEV

No! I demand you complete the execution. I demand that you kill me!

TREPOV

I wish I could — but we make no martyrs here. (*loudly, for the crowd*) You're going to Siberia. (*Trepov signals and the Corporal and two policemen seize Nechaev and march him back downstage to his cell. Trepov follows. The policemen exit and the Corporal takes up a guarding position just inside the door, as Nechaev looks around, puzzled. The other stage lights dim as the stage empties.*)

NECHAEV

Why have you brought me back here?

TREPOV

The Alexis Ravelin Prison is your new home.

NECHAEV

I was exiled to Siberia.

TREPOV

That was for the crowd's benefit. We can't risk your escaping from Siberia like your old friend Bakunin did. (*expansively*) In a way, being imprisoned here is an honor. The Peter and Paul Fortress is the most hallowed spot in Russia. It was founded by Peter the Great as the center of the whole empire. The Imperial Mint is here, and all the Romanoffs are buried right over there in the cathedral.

NECHAEV

This "sacred Fortress" also has two prisons.

TREPOV

Ah, but only the most dangerous are kept here in the Ravelin. It was named after the first prisoner in the Fortress — the Czarevich Alexis.

NECHAEV

The name is appropriate. He was also the first to be beaten to death here — by his own father "Peter the Great."

TREPOV

(*bristling*) Yes, that's an interesting tradition about the Ravelin. (*hard*) Few prisoners leave it alive.

NECHAEV

(*uneasily*) My sentence was —

TREPOV

The Czar changed the sentence.

NECHAEV

To what?

TREPOV

Lifetime confinement in Cell Number 5.

NECHAEV

(*stunned*) He can't do that. I'm entitled to an appeal. The law says —

TREPOV

The Czar is the law.

NECHAEV

(*after a pause, recovering*) Very well, then. If I'm to be a political prisoner, I demand the rights of one. I'll want the usual books, ink, paper . .

TREPOV

No, Number 5. Nothing.

NECHAEV

I'm not "Number 5." I have a name. I am Nechaev.

TREPOV

You have a cell and a cell number. Nothing more. You weren't sent here on a vacation, Number 5. The Ravelin is your tomb. (*smiling as this sinks in*) Goodbye, Number 5. (*Laughing, Trepov exits, but the Corporal hesitates — looking back to see how Nechaev reacts to this.*)

NECHAEV

(*shouting*) Nechaev, Nechaev, Nechaev! (*Nechaev's Gethsemane: the truth of his situation hits him. A sob escapes, and he crumples to a kneeling position on the floor, his head down, wracked and shaking. The Corporal takes a tentative step forward, concerned. Nechaev notices he is still there and fights for control of himself.*) No! I can't let them break me. I won't. I won't! (*He lowers his head again, struggling with himself. When he lifts his face, there are tears on it. The Corporal is moved to pity and looks carefully out the door. Then he crosses to Nechaev, pulling the flute from his pocket. He offers it to Nechaev to make him feel better. Nechaev takes it, and as he studies the tentative smile on the Corporal's face, he begins to comprehend the meaning of the gesture — and its potential! Smiling*) Thank you. That's very kind. (*The Corporal nods shyly, his smile grows, then realizing where he is, he turns and goes out the door, closing it and locking it.*) Of course. Of course. I should have seen it before. This is the Fortress of Saint Peter and Saint Paul. (*He leaps suddenly to his feet, the spotlight comes on him, and he moves to address the audience.*) These Christians have forgotten the New Testament. In Act Three, I'll teach them — and you — the lesson of the Saints in Prison! (*He laughs and begins to play his triumphant tune. The lights fade out.*)

184

ACT THREE

Scene 1

Nechaev's cell. Cyclorama: slide of Duke Urusov. In the darkness, Nechaev's flute is heard playing, then the slide fades up and holds briefly. A spotlight reveals Nechaev in his cell, writing at a small, swing-out table attached to the wall. There are books and papers piled at one end. He finishes writing and lays down his pen. Turning to the audience, he waves the sheet to dry it and puts it in an envelope.

NECHAEV

Act Three. Resurrection and Triumph. With his enemy safely in the tomb, the Czar felt safe to make some changes. (*indicates the table*) This is part of them. Books and writing materials. In exchange for such kindness, Alexander naively expects all prisoners to recant their political heresies. (*indicates the letter*) This is my answer. The first epistle to the Romanoffs. (*grins and turns toward the door*) Guard! (*The Corporal enters and Nechaev holds out the letter.*) For the Czar. (*Bewildered, the corporal takes it and leaves.*) And now, Pentecost in St. Petersburg! (*He signals, and the spotlight dims, or goes out, as the stage lights come up. The slide begins to fade out. A drum rolls and a policeman appears on the ramparts.*)

POLICEMAN

Hear ye. Hear ye. The People will gather to hear a statement by Duke Urusov, newly appointed minister of the interior. (*He exits. Tkachev, Sofia, and Drovnik enter from one direction, and Vera leads in Nickolay Kibalchich from another. He is a thin, short-bearded intellectual in his late twenties. He wears a shabby frock coat and battered, half-crushed top hat. His hair under the hat has a cowlick. He looks and acts like an absent-minded professor. The conspirators themselves all appear older; Drovnik now has a beard. On Vera's arm is a covered basket — which we will see later in another guise! — and from it she takes bundled sheets of propaganda. She hands them to the others as they stand talking downstage. From his cell, Nechaev looks on approvingly.*)

VERA

Comrades, this is Nickolay Kibalchich, a new recruit. He'll help us today. (*Drovnik sticks out his hand. For a moment, Kibalchich does not notice; then he takes it matter-of-factly and pumps it once and drops it. From now on, the conspirators will regard him with tolerant amusement — which will completely escape him.*)

SOFIA

(*cynically*) Is this our new breed of recruit?

VERA

He has special talents we may need. He's trained in both medicine and engineering.

KIBALCHICH

(*nodding*) I'm also a chemist. (*indicates the pamphlets*) This isn't much in my line, but I'm willing to give you a hand passing them out.

SOFIA

Thank you very much.

KIBALCHICH

(*tips his hat*) You're welcome. (*People have begun to drift in.*)

DROVNIK

(*joking*) Well, let's get on with our dirty work.

VERA

Andrei — !

SOFIA

(*takes a bundle*) You'd think six months in jail would have curbed your sense of humor.

DROVNIK

(*smiling*) I'm sorry. I'll try to behave myself — but it will be hard. (*Despite herself, Vera smiles as she gives him a bundle. Tkachev, who has uneasily been watching the crowd gather, now steps up to them.*)

TKACHEV

Vera, I still think this is unwise. Duke Urusov is our ally. To do this during his speech may anger him.

VERA

He'll forgive us. (*gives him a bundle*) And we can't pass up such an opportunity. Take your places. (*The conspirators scatter about the stage, as people continue coming in. Kibalchich stands near Vera, lost in reading one of the handouts. Alexander Ulyanov and his young brother Vladimir enter. Ulyanov is a reserved, intense man in his twenties, and carries schoolbooks under his arm. Young Vladimir is dressed in a schoolboy's uniform and wears wire-rimmed glasses. Alexander sees Kibalchich and crosses down to him.*)

ULYANOV

Niko!

KIBALCHICH

(*momentarily lost*) What? Oh. Alexi. (*He gives him his one-pump handshake.*) How are things at the University?

ULYANOV

They haven't been the same since you were expelled. No one argues with the professors anymore.

THE NIHILIST

KIBALCHICH

(*to Vera*) This is Alexi Ulyanov. He's a student of zoology. Alexi, this is Vera . . Vera . . (*He has forgotten her cover name.*)

VERA

(*shaking hands*) Petrovich.

ULYANOV

(*pulling in Vladimir*) My brother Vladimir. He came in today from Simbursk to take the entrance examinations for the University.

VERA

Another zoologist?

VLADIMIR

I'm going to be a lawyer — like Duke Urusov.

ULYANOV

Urusov is his hero. That's why we're here — to listen to this big announcement. (*to Kibalchich*) Why are you here? You've never been fond of ceremonies like this. (*Kibalchich looks uneasily at Vera and she nods for him to take Ulyanov aside and explain. He finally understands and does so — in pantomime, giving Ulyanov a propaganda sheet to make the point clear. Vladimir stands awkwardly with Vera, who studies him noncommittally. There is a short pause.*)

VLADIMIR

Ah . . are you supporters of the Duke?

VERA

We endorse what he's trying to do.

VLADIMIR

(*beaming*) So do thousands of others. His reform party grows stronger every day. Someday, he'll win us a constitutional government.

VERA

(*dryly*) It's nice to think so. (*Stung a little, he frowns and starts to ask what she means, but his brother returns and takes his arm to lead him away.*)

ULYANOV

Come along, Vladimir. These people are busy.

VLADIMIR

Busy . . ?

ULYANOV

(*over his shoulder*) Good luck, comrades. (*They move to the other side of the now-gathered crowd, but Vladimir still looks back, puzzled.*)

KIBALCHICH

Alexi won't give us away. He sympathizes with us. Given time, I think I could persuade him to join us.

VERA

There will be time for that later. We may want a group inside the University. (*A drum sounds.*) Get ready. Here he comes. (*Attention turns to the ramparts where Urusov appears in his robes of state. The crowd cheers and continues to cheer and applaud as is appropriate in his speech. Trepov and a policeman appear, followed by the Major, and stand to one side on the ramparts watching. As the Duke speaks, the conspirators quietly pass out the sheets to the crowd.*)

DUKE

His Majesty Alexander the Second, Emperor and Autocrat of all the Russias, makes the following proclamation. (*He unrolls a scroll and reads.*) "Be it hereby ordained by our decree that a new era of good will shall exist in our lands and hold dominion over all our citizens. The recent stringent security measures, now unnecessary, shall be repealed. The Office of Censor is abolished and the Third Division is hereby dissolved. Repentant political prisoners shall gain our amnesty, and all political refugees are asked to return to their Mother Russia where they will be welcomed with forbearance and forgiving. All students expelled for political reasons shall be pardoned and reinstated upon taking an oath of fealty. Be it further known that an era of official reform is now begun and shall continue so long as law and order shall prevail. We appeal to our subjects to dwell in peace and brotherhood. So set forth by our hand this day, Czar Alexander." (*During this, the Major has seen the distribution and pointed it out to Trepov, who has ordered him to make an arrest. The Major leaves the ramparts with the policeman, and they circle around and come in behind the crowd to arrest Drovnik, as the speech ends, and the Duke bows, basking in the applause. Drovnik resists, and the crowd stops applauding to watch as the policeman handcuffs Drovnik and drags him along behind the Major to the foot of the ramparts. The Major hands up a copy of the sheet to Trepov, who looks at it and smiles. The Duke is upset.*) What's going on here? Why are you arresting that man?

TREPOV

(*giving him the sheet*) He was passing out revolutionary propaganda. Your "Era of Good Will" was short-lived.

DUKE

(*glancing at it*) I find nothing revolutionary in this. It calls for reform. That's why the Czar appointed me.

TREPOV

It also calls for a constitution and an elected parliament of the people.

DUKE

Which the Czar may one day grant. The day of you reactionaries is over.

THE NIHILIST

(*to crowd*) Long live the Era of Good Will! Long live the Czar! (*Relieved, the crowd cheers and various members repeat the two phrases. Trepov angrily signals the policeman to take away Drovnik, but the Duke notices. So does the crowd, and it falls silent.*) Where are you taking him?

TREPOV

To the Fortress — for questioning.

DUKE

No! None of your tortures. He's to be turned loose. Do you hear me? Free him! Now! (*For a moment, there is a staring, silent clash of wills — but the Duke is Trepov's superior, and finally, irate but obeying, Trepov signals the policeman, and Drovnik is freed.*)

DROVNIK

Long live the Duke!

CROWD

(*various*) Long live the Duke!

DROVNIK

(*timing it well*) And to hell with Trepov! (*He gives Trepov the finger and sprints offstage, the policeman right behind him. The crowd laughs and cheers; some echo the cry. The Duke leaves, triumphant and smiling, and the crowd drifts out. Trepov scowls down on them, then stalks out with the Major behind. The conspirators gather downstage; Ulyanov and Vladimir watch carefully from a distance.*)

SOFIA

(*to Tkachev*) There, you see! The Duke is on our side.

TKACHEV

But why take chances? Give him a chance to make his reforms.

VERA

The government moves too slowly. We plan to give it a push.

TKACHEV

(*shaking his head*) What will it take to convince you? You're playing right into Trepov's hands. (*As if in affirmation, the policeman roughly pulls a once more handcuffed Drovnik across the stage. Trepov and the Major enter below to greet them.*)

TREPOV

(*enjoying himself*) So . . the hound has caught the hare. Tell me, rabbit, why are you still an agitator in this "Era of Good Will?"

DROVNIK

(*joking right back*) You know how it is, General. Some people are never satisfied.

TREPOV

(*dropping the mask*) You insolent clown — ! I'll teach you respect. (*to policeman*) Take him inside.

MAJOR

General, are you sure this is wise? Remember the Duke's orders.

TREPOV

And you would do well to remember you work for me now. I'm not disobeying the Duke. I'll turn him loose — (*hard*) after I've taught him some manners. (*He gestures for them to go inside, and they exit. The conspirators stir uneasily.*)

TKACHEV

I warned you — but you wouldn't listen. You had to provoke trouble. This is what happens when you act like fools. (*There is the sound of a lash and a yell. The conspirators react, and their next lines are played in counterpoint to the rest of ten lashes. Ulyanov and Vladimir react, too, with Alexander growing more and more angry.*)

SOFIA

They're beating him!

VERA

(*bitterly*) This is their "Era of Good Will"!

KIBALCHICH

Trepov will never change.

VERA

And neither will the government — until men like him are eliminated.

TKACHEV

What are you saying?

SOFIA

Andrei must be avenged!

TKACHEV

(*desperately, fearing their line of thought*) All right, we'll go to Urusov. He'll punish Trepov for this.

KIBALCHICH

The Czar would never allow it. Trepov is one of his pets.

VERA

Then it's up to us.

TKACHEV

Have you forgotten what violence led to before? Have you forgotten Nechaev? (*The beating has ended, and Drovnik's moans subside.*)

VERA

(*in the quiet*) I remember him now. (*Nechaev smiles in his cell. Drovnik staggers in, walking very carefully, trying not to wince or cry out at the pain. He reaches the conspirators and sinks to his knees. Sofia and Vera ease him down; the back of his shirt is bloody rags. Ulyanov is drawn to the group and grimaces at what he sees. Vladimir tugs at his arm, trying to pull him away.)*

VLADIMIR

Alexi! Come home with me. Don't get involved with this.

ULYANOV

(enraged, pointing to Drovnik) How can I help myself? Look for yourself.

VLADIMIR

(looks, reacts, and changes his stand) You're right. What can we do?

ULYANOV

(suddenly) No! Not you. Me! *(shoves the books at him)* You go on home. Study for your exams. This cause doesn't need you.

VLADIMIR

(hurt) But Alexi . . !

ULYANOV

One Ulyanov in this is enough. Go on! Get out! *(Vladimir leaves, looking backward unhappily. Kibalchich pats Alexander's shoulder, and they turn to where Sofia sits stroking Drovnik's head while Vera looks helplessly at his torn back.)*

SOFIA

Poor fool. Poor brave fool.

VERA

I should have known. I should have known.

TKACHEV

(trying to take command) We'll have to move carefully from now on. Trepov will be watching for any mistakes. We can't take any chances.

SOFIA

(hard) We must take any chance we can.

ULYANOV

There won't be justice for anyone until tyrants like Trepov are overthrown.

KIBALCHICH

(matter-of-factly) Or killed.

TKACHEV

(as the others nod) Are you mad? Assassination would mean the end of everything.

VERA

(almost calmly, decided) Trepov must die! *(The lights blink out on the group downstage, and Nechaev stands smiling in his spotlight.)*

191

NECHAEV

And such are the first-fruits of my Pentecost. For your catechism: Luke, Chapter 21, verses 22 to 26. "These be the days of vengeance, that all things written be fulfilled. Woe unto them that are with child, and to them that give suck in these days! For there shall be a great distress in the land and wrath upon this people. They shall fall by the edge of the sword. And there shall be signs in the sun and in the moon and in the stars; the sea and the waves shall roar, and upon the earth, nations distressed with perplexity. Men's hearts shall fail them in fear as they see the things which are coming on earth — and the powers of heaven shall be shaken!" (*He laughs and begins to play a strong, determined melody — his victory theme, or perhaps the "Internationale"? Cyclorama: slide of Alexander II holds during following. The lights suddenly flash on in Nechaev's cell, and the Corporal throws open the cell door, his face frightened. Nechaev stops playing and turns as two policemen enter, seize him, and chain his wrists. That chain is then tethered to the wall, giving him some freedom to move — but not much. They take the books and writing materials and exit.*) What are you doing? What do you think you're doing? (*Trepov enters, playing with a letter.*) Is this your idea?

TREPOV

(*holds up the letter*) It is the Czar's. He didn't like your letter criticizing him. He gave me the honor of personally carrying our your punishment. (*Nechaev struggles to reach him, leaning against the tether — but Trepov laughingly keeps just out of reach.*)

NECHAEV

You arrogant bastard! (*Trepov slaps Nechaev with the letter.*)

TREPOV

Number 5, we've heard enough from you. Your punishment is chains and silence. From this moment on, no one will ever speak to you again. And you will live in those chains until the day you die.

NECHAEV

You'll be punished for this. I will have revenge.

TREPOV

(*elaborately*) That's strange. I thought I heard something. I must have been mistaken. (*He exits, laughing, fanning himself with the letter.*)

NECHAEV

Damn you, Trepov! I'll have your life for this! Damn you! Damn you! (*The Corporal quickly closes the cell door and locks it. Nechaev shakes his fists in his chains, and the cell lights fade out as he struggles with the chains. Cyclorama: the Czar slide fades out.*)

Scene 2

Outside the Ravelin. Clyclorama: slide — an apple. Fades out. As the lights come up, the Major is examining an apple from the basket of an old peddler woman — a bent, old crone in glasses with gray hair showing under a long, concealing shawl. Trepov enters, slapping the letter into his gloved hand, followed at a respectful distance by two policemen. Trepov joins the Major, pocketing the letter. The two policemen automatically move in on either side as Trepov takes an apple from the woman and examines it for bruises.

MAJOR

How did it go?

TREPOV

He'll give us no more trouble. (*He hands the peddler a coin, but she drops it. The Major and the two policemen start to stoop for it, and the "old woman" suddenly produces a knife from under her shawl.*)

VERA

Sic semper tyrannis! (*She plunges the knife into Trepov, who falls, screaming. The Major kneels beside him. The two policemen quickly seize Vera and take the bloody knife from her with no difficulty. As she is handcuffed, she stares down transfixed at Trepov who moans weakly while the Major examines him.*)

MAJOR

(*standing, to the policemen*) Carry him inside — quickly! (*They carry Trepov out, and the Major studies the assassin for a moment, then pulls down the shawl and removes the gray wig and glasses to reveal Vera. He smiles.*) Your name is Zasner. Vera Zasner. You were Nechaev's mistress. Why did you stab Trepov?

VERA

I have nothing to say.

MAJOR

You knife spoke most eloquently.

VERA

What are you going to do with me?

MAJOR

(*wryly*) First, perhaps I should thank you.

VERA

What — ?

MAJOR

You've restored me. Now the Czar will listen to me again. This will finish

193

Urusov and his liberals and put the Third Division right back in business. (*to Vera*) You didn't think of that as a consequence, did you?

VERA

I didn't care.

MAJOR

That's the trouble with revolutionaries. Too little logic.

VERA

That's the trouble with men like you. Too much of it. If you had one ounce of compassion, you'd have stabbed Trepov yourself.

MAJOR

I already have — in my own way. A report on his violations of the Czar's decree is on the Duke's desk right now. But it doesn't matter anymore. When the Czar finds out about this, the truce is over. Thanks to your grand act of passion, the war is on again. (*Shaking his head, he leads her out. At one side, the Corporal has been an astounded witness to the scene — and he stands stunned as the lights fade down to leave him illuminated alone. Nechaev creeps out of the darkness behind him, standing on the edge of the light in his chains.*)

NECHAEV

You see? I said it would happen. One of my comrades has avenged me. Why do you resist our cause? Join us. I can see you get rewards. (*The Corporal shakes his head. He will not look at Nechaev, but he is listening.*) You're a prisoner, too. The state keeps you in chains as strong as mine. This prison is your whole life. You work here, eat here, sleep here. Once a month, they give you a few rubles and let you romp with the whores in town. No decent girl will even look at you. And who are your friends? (*The Corporal stirs uneasily.*) You're a good man, a kind man, but how do people treat you when you tell them your profession? They fear you. They act like you have the pox. We are comrades, you and I. Prisoners of the Czar. We must help each other. (*Weakening, the Corporal shakes his head.*) My time is coming, Corporal. The Revolution draws nearer every day. The People support my cause. Watch! (*Nechaev gestures, and the lights come up on the courtroom above them. The Judge is in his usual place, and Duke Urusov stands beside Vera at the prisoner's dock. Between them sits a weakened Trepov. No one else is present, and the scene is almost a surrealistic vision created by Nechaev. At the Judge's first words, the Corporal turns to watch. Cyclorama: slide — the Romanoff Imperial Eagles.*)

JUDGE

(*gaveling*) The court will hear closing argument for the defense. Duke Urusov. (*The Duke comes forward and begins to pantomime his speech. It is clear that his arguments concern Trepov, as the General bristles. Below, the Corporal watches entranced.*)

NECHAEV

See? Urusov himself is defending her. The Czar forced him to resign as minister of the interior because he was too lenient with the People. For revenge, the Duke now carries out our will. (*Urusov has finished and sits down. The Judge gavels.*)

JUDGE

The jury will consider its verdict.

NECHAEV

(*to the Corporal*) The government is so confident of the outcome they've even allowed a trial by jury. But see the choice the People make. Trepov or the revolutionary. (*The Judge produces a piece of paper and opens it.*)

JUDGE

Vera Zasner, the jury finds you — (*He stops, not believing what he sees.*)

NECHAEV

(*finishing*) Not guilty! (*He laughs, and the lights blink out on the courtroom. Cyclorama: the Romanoff Eagles dissolve into Nechaev. To the Corporal*) There is your answer. The People have chosen. The class war has begun, and the aristocracy is doomed! All who oppose us will die! Join us, Corporal. Join us now — because it's coming. It's coming. (*shouting*) Revolution! (*Cyclorama: slides of a period Russian train flash on here and there, larger and larger, timed to the following, until they show an explosion and a wreck. This might also be done with a slide-film combination. As Nechaev speaks the words above, the sound of a train is heard approaching, growing louder. On the word "Revolution," Nechaev throws his chained fists in the air and a European train whistle screams. It holds long and loud — nearer and nearer — until there is a gigantic explosion and the grinding roar of a wreck. Cyclorama: the Nechaev slide is alone in darkness above the stage. The lights go out, and Nechaev laughs in the dark, wildly, maniacally. This may be taped for best effect. As his laughter begins to die, it is picked up by the following scene.*)

Scene 3

Sofia and Drovnik's room. Cyclorama: the Nechaev slide is very dim. We hear the laughter of the conspirators, their cries of "Happy New Year," and a party horn blowing. The lights come up on the meagerly furnished room shared by Sofia and Drovnik. The two of them are helping Vera and Ulyanov off with their coats. Drovnik blows his little party horn at Vera. Kibalchich sits at a table, totally absorbed in tinkering with the mechanism of a music box. Tkachev stands gloomily alone in a corner — tired and drawn — on the very edge of sanity. The room has a few pitiful streamers of paper hung for decoration, perhaps a card with "1881" on it, and there are glasses and a bottle of vodka on the table. Sofia hangs up the coats.

VERA

(*to the others*) You remember Alexi Ulyanov. He has his own group at the University now.

DROVNIK

Welcome. (*pours him a drink*) You honor our home.

ULYANOV

Thank you. (*to Kibalchich*) Niko, what are you playing with? A music box?

KIBALCHICH

(*coming to*) Hm? Oh, yes. Someday, one of these may help us blow up a building. (*He lets the music box play a moment, then flips shut the lid with a bang.*)

VERA

That's why I brought Alexi along with me — to learn such tricks from you. He has a scientist's interest in things that go BOOM! (*Everyone but Tkachev laughs. Drovnik takes out his pistol and gavels with it on the table.*)

DROVNIK

Sit down. Sit down. Let's get the meeting started. (*Everyone sits but Tkachev who stays where he is.*) Now I know I'm supposed to lead this group, but technically Vera outranks me. And having lived with Sofia for eighteen months, I know better than to haggle with a revolutionary female. So I'm stepping aside in favor of our National Coordinator. (*He leads the others in applause, and, smiling, Vera moves to the head of the table to replace him. She takes up his pistol from the table and gavels with it.*)

VERA

As National Coordinator of the People's Will, I call this meeting to order. Reports.

SOFIA

This has been the most successful year in our history. We've killed or wounded dozens of officials. The Czar himself barely escaped our attempt upon the Imperial Train.

TKACHEV

There were others who didn't escape.

VERA

(*turning*) What?

TKACHEV

Two of our comrades were captured after the wreck. Now they're prisoners

196

in the Ravelin . . (*crossing to face them at the table*) and they're going
to die!

TKACHEV → VERA

(*gaveling*) Comrade, you don't have the floor. You're out of order.

TKACHEV

Order? For a parliament of anarchists?!

VERA

(*gaveling*) Please sit down.

TKACHEV

Why won't you listen? Can't you see we'll all end up dead? The police
hound us day and night.

KIBALCHICH

Not tonight. It's New Year's Eve.

DROVNIK

Everyone is having parties.

SOFIA

Don't be a scold, Tkachev.

VERA

We all know the price of revolution.

TKACHEV

Well, I'm not willing to pay it. I've had enough blood.

DROVNIK

What are you trying to say?

TKACHEV

I can't live with this violence any longer. It's driving me insane. I can't
eat. I can't sleep. (*pointing at them*) I see death-heads on all your faces.
I'm afraid to look in a mirror for fear I'll see one on my own. I want
to resign.

VERA

(*rising, a warning*) Tkachev — !

TKACHEV

Don't worry. I'll go where there's no danger of betraying you. I'm leaving
Russia to go into exile.

VERA

(*a pause, looking at him, then*) Your resignation is accepted. (*She gavels
once and sits. She does not look at him again.*)

TKACHEV

Is that all you have to say?

VERA

We're sorry to lose you, of course. You've been with us a long time. But
you've grown weak. You were becoming a threat to us. We're pleased you

solved a difficult problem for us. (*The others nod, looking stonily at Tkachev. He is already a stranger now, an outsider, and he suddenly realizes how close he's been to death at their hands.*)

TKACHEV

You meant to kill me — !

VERA

It makes no difference now. Your decision was a good one for all of us.

TKACHEV

You're as mad as he was. You're all as bad as Nechaev. Lunatics! Damned! (*Vera rises slowly, the pistol held now for possible use, but not in a threatening way — merely ready.*)

VERA

(*a dismissal*) Goodbye, Tkachev. (*He stares at her a moment, at the pistol, then leaves, grabbing his coat and fleeing into the darkness. Vera stands a moment, staring straight ahead, then sits — her coldness easing. The atmosphere at the table improves immediately.*) Other reports. Alexi.

ULYANOV

My group at the University plans to use the laboratories to make bombs and acid for our work. We'd like to coordinate our efforts with this group.

DROVNIK

We plan to try for the Czar again. Can your group make us some bombs?

ULYANOV

If Niko shows me how.

KIBALCHICH

That won't be necessary now. You get me the ingredients and I'll make them here. I've come across an interesting formula for making something called "nitroglycerine." It was in the *Russian Artillery Journal* for August 1878.

SOFIA

Spare us the details, comrade. We know you'll make it work.

KIBALCHICH

(*missing her jibe*) Thank you. That's very flattering.

SOFIA

Our plan is to attack the Czar on his way to the Sunday military parade. We've rented a shop on the route to the ceremony. We'll tunnel under the street and explode one of Niko's wonders as the Czar's carriage goes by.

VERA

And if he uses another street?

DROVNIK

Others of us will be ready with bombs.

THE NIHILIST

KIBALCHICH

Actually, they'll be more like grenades. Nitroglycerine will let me make them smaller. Easier to throw, more accuracy.

VERA

Just as powerful?

KIBALCHICH

(*a bit offended*) Of course.

SOFIA

The Czar won't escape us this time.

DROVNIK

I hope the Czar prays well in church Sunday morning.

ULYANOV

Why?

DROVNIK

He's going to face God Himself by Sunday night. (*He laughs, and the others join in.*)

VERA

I'll see to it that pamphlets are prepared to tell the People why the Czar died. Alexi, we'll use your group to distribute them.

ULYANOV

I'd rather handle the bombs.

VERA

Patience, comrade. You'll get your chance. Any other business? (*Drovnik seizes the bottle and begins pouring drinks.*)

DROVNIK

I move we adjourn. (*The others hold forth glasses with cries of* "Second the motion.")

VERA

(*laughs and gavels*) Adjourned. (*The group relaxes. Drovnik pours drinks. Kibalchich demonstrates the music box to Ulyanov. Suddenly, there is a knock at the door and everyone freezes. There is a pause, then the knock is repeated. Vera begins to act: she slides the pistol to Drovnik, who holds it at the ready under his jacket. She then takes up her drink and signals Sofia to the door. Firmly*) We're having a party. (*Sofia crosses and opens the door. The Corporal enters. He looks at them fearfully, removing his cap in respect, licking his lips.*)

SOFIA

(*uncertainly*) What do you want?

CORPORAL

Sofia Perovna?

SOFIA

(*slowly, after a pause*) Yes . . (*He hands her a note, and she reads it, her eyes widening.*) It's from Nechaev! He's alive — in the Ravelin! (*There are exclamations of amazement from the group.*)

CORPORAL

(*proudly*) I'm his guard.

VERA

(*suspicious*) How did you get this address?

CORPORAL

From the ones who blew up the Czar's train. They're in the same cell block. (*proudly*) I introduced them to Nechaev.

DROVNIK

Do you work for Nechaev?

CORPORAL

(*a bit hurt*) I work for the Revolution. We are comrades. (*proudly*) I'm helping him organize the other guards. (*The conspirators react — first in amazement, then in glee.*)

ULYANOV

Amazing!

DROVNIK

Not for Nechaev!

SOFIA

(*reading*) He asks that we give this man some money so that he can use it in the prison.

CORPORAL

(*proudly*) I'll be Nechaev's messenger to you. (*Drovnik gets a glass and pours a drink for the Corporal.*)

DROVNIK

A toast. To the best news of the new year.

SOFIA

Nechaev!

ALL (BUT VERA)

Nechaev! (*Vera stands thinking as the others drink. The Corporal drains his glass and holds it out for more. Drovnik pours him another drink — and the Corporal beams, obviously unused to such treatment.*)

CORPORAL

Nechaev said you would treat me well. (*He takes a big drink.*)

KIBALCHICH

Good news is always welcome.

VERA

How many of the guards have joined you?

THE NIHILIST

CORPORAL

All of the ones in the Ravelin, and nearly half of those in the rest of the Fortress.

VERA

Does he plan to escape?

SOFIA

No one has ever escaped from the Fortress.

CORPORAL

Nechaev can. He has a complete map of the Fortress with an escape route all planned. But he doesn't want to escape. (*They lean forward, intent to learn why, but he playfully holds out his empty glass, and Drovnik impatiently fills it. The Corporal takes a drink.*) Nechaev has a plan to capture the Czar. (*The conspirators react with skepticism.*) He does. He says the Czar feels safe only in the Fortress. He prays there on Sundays in the cathedral. Nechaev plans to lead the guards and capture him. We can hold the Czar in the Fortress and rule all Russia from there. (*The sheer incredibility stuns them for a moment, then they begin to react.*)

SOFIA

Incredible!

DROVNIK

I wager he'd try it.

CORPORAL

(*looking around*) Will you help us? (*The conspirators quiet, then turn to look at Vera. She slowly shakes her head.*)

VERA

We have other plans. Nechaev will have to wait.

CORPORAL

He won't like that.

VERA

He'll understand. Destroying the Czar comes first.

DROVNIK

(*filling his glass again*) Here, have another drink. We have much to celebrate tonight.

CORPORAL

(*holding up his glass in a shaky hand*) To Nechaev, the Eagle of the Revolution.

VERA

To success in the new year.

CORPORAL

Happy New Year! (*The others laugh and drink, echoing the cry as the lights fade out on the room, leaving a dim light on the street downstage.*

201

From the shadows there, the Major appears alone, looking in the direction of the party — then steps back out of sight. The Corporal staggers into the light and carefully makes his way lurching along the street, holding his head and trying to navigate. He disappears finally, and the Major steps out to look after him, thinking, then decides to follow him. The lights fade out.)

Scene 4

The Ravelin. Cyclorama: slide of Alexander II; another of two bags of groceries. Holds a moment, then fades. The lights come up on the cell, where Nechaev paces nervously. The Corporal enters, very hungover and moving carefully, crosses to the cell, and enters. Nechaev practically pounces on him.

NECHAEV

Well, what news? Did you find them? Did they send money? Messages?

CORPORAL

(*sagging against the wall, holding his head*) Comrade, please! I don't feel so well. (*hands him a packet*) There. It's all in there. (*Nechaev opens the packet and finds a handful of paper money, some pamphlets, and a letter. He shouts with joy, seizes the Corporal, and swings him around. The Corporal breaks free.*) Comrade, please . . !

NECHAEV

Did they tell you their plan?

CORPORAL

They're laying an ambush with a mine and bombs. It's a good plan.

NECHAEV

Mine is better. You and I have nearly all the guards on our side.

CORPORAL

They said they didn't want to take the chance. If one guard talked, they'd walk into a trap.

NECHAEV

Will they help us escape, then?

CORPORAL

(*nodding*) After their attempt on the Czar.

NECHAEV

Then when the Czar is dead, I live again. The Messiah of Revolution will rise from the tomb! (*The Corporal grimaces at Nechaev's shouts, and Nechaev laughs, sits down, and takes out his flute. He begins to play a tense, threatening tune. Holding his head, the Corporal exits. Above, Drovnik and Sofia leave their room, separate, and cross the stage, carrying bags of what look like groceries. A loaf of bread sticks out of one and celery stalks from the other. They take up their stations, waiting. After a moment, the Major saunters in alone, his eyes searching, his face intent. Seeing him, Drovnik climbs up over the ramparts and exits. Curious, the Major climbs up to look after him. Sofia, who has remained still, now exits quickly downstage. The Major notices, and his concern deepens. He takes one last unhappy look around, then hurries out. Nechaev continues to play the tense, threatening tune on his flute. The sky darkens, and the set becomes a black bulk against the cyclorama's blue. Suddenly, there is a brilliant flash and the sound of an explosion. Nechaev stops playing and leaps to his feet. There is another flash and explosion, and the sky turns red and the entire stage is bathed in blood-red light. Nechaev raises his fists and roars. Cyclorama: slides — one after another — of the bloody Alexander on his deathbed, from the famous painting. Each should be a closer shot, until the Czar's bloody face is seen in closeup. All may be on the cyclorama at the same time. The Major hurries in and looks toward the slides. The stage lighting begins to lose its red coloring. A battered Trepov staggers in, his uniform torn and spattered with blood. The Major meets him and helps him sit down.)*

MAJOR

What happened?

TREPOV

Assassins! We got your warning and took another street — but they were waiting there, too. They attacked us by the canal. The first bomb missed — but wounded a little boy. The Czar insisted on stopping to see how he was. Then a second bomb was thrown. (*He buries his face in his hands.*)

MAJOR

The Czar! What happened to the Czar?

TREPOV

He was on his hands and knees in a pool of blood, his uniform in rags, and his legs . . his legs , . (*He cannot continue.*)

MAJOR

Is he dead?

TREPOV

He's dying. We couldn't stop the flow of blood. We left a trail of blood all the way to the palace.

MAJOR

(*anguished*) Why didn't you make him go on after the first bomb missed?

TREPOV

I tried — but he was worried about the little boy. It grieved him to think the boy had been hurt by a bomb meant for him. Major, he's not the cold, remote monarch some people think he is. He really cares about his people. He cares — and it's killed him! (*The scene is shattered as Nechaev suddenly appears near them in his spotlight, wrists still chained but no longer tethered to his cell wall.*)

NECHAEV

(*angrily*) Enough! No sympathy here for the Czar. You're out of character, Trepov. Get hold of yourself and get on with the play.

TREPOV

(*still shaken*) What kind of monster are you?

NECHAEV

The death of kings leaves me unmoved. (*points toward the Ravelin*) Continue!

TREPOV

(*shaking his head*) You make a mockery of everything human.

NECHAEV

You're no man to talk about humanity.

TREPOV

(*struggling to his feet*) But I *am* human. I have a family I love. I laugh, I cry, I bleed! It's you who make me a lie. It's your story which makes me the same kind of fiend as you.

NECHAEV

(*warning*) Trepov . .

TREPOV

(*desperately*) It's not true. You're making me a lie.

NECHAEV

It serves my purpose.

TREPOV

(*seizing on this*) Yes, you have to make me evil, don't you? So you can appear righteous. To give you meaning and purpose. Revolutionaries must have villains to hate — or they cannot exist!

NECHAEV

(*slaps him*) Damn you, play the scene! (*Trepov reels under the blow. The Major stands silently watching.*)

TREPOV

(*moaning*) I'll make you sorry. I'll make you sorry. (*Nechaev signals, and a bell begins a slow tolling.*)

NECHAEV

The Czar is dead. Now play it to the end. Our final confrontation, Trepov. Your great moment — and mine. (*Trepov staggers into the Ravelin. The Major stands watching. To the audience*) For a moment there, he was almost a man. (*He sees the major; hard*) Well — ? (*As if he has decided something, the Major strides off into the Ravelin. Nechaev crosses directly to his cell.*

204

THE NIHILIST

After a moment, as the lights come up, the door opens. Trepov enters, and for a moment, the two men stand there, staring at each other. Trepov is now in control of himself, hard and cold and full of hate.) There is blood on you, General. Your own, I hope. *(Trepov says nothing; Nechaev indicates the bell.)* The Czar is dead, isn't he? *(meaning Trepov)* Who knows who will be next? *(Trepov nods, but he means something else!)* Did you come here to tell me personally the Czar is dead? I'm honored that you think me so important.

TREPOV

I have another message for you. The nation is now under martial law. The police have taken charge of all government functions — including prisons.

NECHAEV

(uneasily) For how long?

TREPOV

Long enough. *(After a short pause as this sinks in, the Corporal suddenly flies into the room and sprawls on the floor. He no longer wears his military blouse but a plain prison shirt. The Major enters and stands just inside the door. To the Corporal)* Go stand in the corner, Number 5. *(The Corporal scrambles into the corner and cowers there. Nechaev looks at him with growing comprehension and horror. To Nechaev)* Yes, we know about your plan. He confessed. You know, you're quite remarkable. You corrupted this prison right under the eyes of its officials.

NECHAEV

(defiantly) It wasn't difficult. Forgotten half-wits for guards. Abuse and cruelty by their officers. Low pay. Loneliness. It was only a matter of time. And I had plenty of that.

TREPOV

But not much more.

NECHAEV

What — ?

TREPOV

For your hard work and great success, we're giving you a promotion. You're no longer Number 5. That honor belongs to your chief helper here. *(indicates the Corporal)* You, nihilist, are now Number 1.

NECHAEV

The punishment cell — !

TREPOV

A private room on the side passage all to yourself. No one will bother you there — ever again.

NECHAEV

You're sending me there to die!

TREPOV

Unfortunately, the budget only allows its occupant twenty-four kopecks of food a day.

NECHAEV

I'll starve — !

TREPOV

(*the ferocity finally blazes forth*) Yes! Your body will begin to swell and fester, and your skin will turn blue. You'll strangle on the stench of your own rot, and your tongue will writhe in your mouth like a bloated, black snake. You'll scream and plead, but no one will come. No one will help. No one but Death — and he'll take his time. That's your fate, nihilist. Does it frighten you?

NECHAEV

(*calm now*) I wouldn't give you the satisfaction. Face it, General. You can't defeat me. You can kill me — but I'll die laughing at you. Because I know I'm going to win. (*He turns and crosses to the Corporal, taking him by the shoulders, straightening him.*) Comrade, I go to die. You are the last friendly face I'll see — and the last to hear my words. Tell everyone you can what happened to me. Tell them I died bravely, unbroken. Tell them my spirit will live on in the Revolution. The Eagle will fly on new wings. Tell them the Revolution will succeed! (*The Corporal nods, gaining new strength from Nechaev. He stops sobbing. Nechaev pats him on the shoulder, smiles, and turns for the door where Trepov and the Major are waiting.*)

CORPORAL

Nechaev! (*Nechaev stops, and the Corporal gets the flute and gives it to him. For a long moment, Nechaev looks at it, then he embraces the Corporal.*)

TREPOV

A flute won't save you. Come!

NECHAEV

(*to the Corporal*) Remember! Nechaev and the Revolution! (*The Corporal nods, and, head high, Nechaev turns and strides out past Trepov and the Major, who follow him. The Corporal looks after them as the door slowly closes, and the lights slowly fade out. Cyclorama: slide — Nechaev's flute. Holds behind the following. In the darkness, Nechaev's flute plays a weak and mournful tune. From a part of the set structure, which doubles as a gallows, four ropes are mounted and swing. Dark figures begin moving onto the stage — the crowd gathering for the execution of the conspirators. It includes Duke Urusov — now aged and slow, leaning heavily upon his cane. Vera, now in glasses and shawl, a fully mature woman, enters with Vladimir, who now has a scraggly goatee and wears a suit. He stands with her, taut and trembling, bitterness written on him, no longer a schoolboy but an intense and angry young man. Policemen take their positions for crowd control and to handle the execution. Nechaev's flute plays more slowly, then falters and stops in mid-phrase. Cyclorama: the flute slide fades out to match the above. Trepov enters during the process, as the lights sneak up to counterbalance the fading slide. He regards the gallows with pleasure. The Major enters, looking somewhat disturbed, and joins Trepov on the ramparts. The lights are now up full, and the slide has disappeared.)*

TREPOV

(turning to the Major) Well . . ? *(For a moment, the Major just stares at him — still shaken by what he's just seen — then he holds up Nechaev's flute. Trepov takes it, laughing; the Major does not like his reaction.)* That's twenty-four kopecks less I'll have to spend. I'll need the money. Our cells are full.

MAJOR

I'm sure you and the Czar will find a way to empty them. *(indicates the gallows)* Like that.

TREPOV

Alexander the Third wants to make an example of them. He intends to keep a firm hand on the people.

MAJOR

(cynically) And we're to be his fingers.

TREPOV

That's very good. His fingers. Yes, you are the pointing finger — and I am the thumb which crushes the windpipe. Together, we've crushed this Revolution.

MAJOR

We haven't captured Vera Zasner.

TREPOV

We will. We nearly had her when we caught Ulyanov. Besides, what can one woman do?

MAJOR

She can keep the fires of revolution going.

TREPOV

(scoffing) How? We're in complete control now. Let one agitator raise his voice, let one demonstrator wave a sign — and we exterminate him!

MAJOR

Wouldn't it be better to exterminate the *causes* of rebellion? Treat the disease instead of the symptoms.

TREPOV

That's not my job. I'm a fireman, not a doctor. And I've put out the fires of this revolution.

MAJOR

Perhaps. Or maybe they're merely banked for a time. Awaiting new fuel. (*Irritated by his tone and attitude, Trepov frowns at him, but the Major meets his frown with a calm and steady look in return. There is the sound of a drum roll, and Trepov has to turn away. Drovnik, Sofia, Kibalchich, and Ulyanov are led in, and taken to low stools or benches which have been placed under the four ropes. They mount them and stand waiting, their hands bound behind them. They wear special white execution robes with hoods, which are now hanging in front above signs which say "Czaricide." The hoods are cut so that they can be put over their heads once the nooses are in place, and are not connected in back but in front. An Orthodox Priest has followed them in and stands near them with a large cross. The four policemen take their places behind and slightly to one side of the benches. Trepov crosses to stand next to the gallows and reads aloud. Cyclorama: slide of Alexander III. Holds for Trepov's speech.*)

TREPOV

Andrei Drovnik, Sofia Perovna, Nickolay Kibalchich, Alexander Ulyanov, you have been found guilty of czaricide, treason, and conspiracy — and you have been sentenced to hang. Let all subjects of His Majesty Czar Alexander the Third know your crimes and know your punishment. May God have mercy on your souls. (*Cyclorama: the slide fades out. Trepov folds the paper and pockets it. The priest moves along the conspirators with the cross, holding it up to them. Drovnik and Sofia turn their heads away from it. Kibalchich kisses it. Ulyanov looks straight ahead until the priest gives up and moves away, to stand for a moment and make the Orthodox sign of the cross toward them. Then he nods to Trepov and begins to pray. Trepov signals, and the policemen step on the benches behind the condemned and pull the ropes down around their necks, then pull the hoods up over their heads. As the hoods are put on, the conspirators cry out.*)

ULYANOV

Down with the Czar!

SOFIA

Down with tyranny!

DROVNIK

Long live the Revolution! (*Trepov raises his hand, and the drum begins to roll, mounting in volume. The policemen now stand behind the condemned on the platform, one foot on the benches. The priest prays furiously on his knees. Trepov drops his hand, the drum stops, and the policemen kick the benches out from under the conspirators. The crowd below gasps; one woman screams.*)

THE NIHILIST

VLADIMIR

Alexi! (*The swinging bodies struggle for a moment, then sway lifelessly. The priest crosses himself, stands up, takes his cross, and goes out. The crowd drifts away, and after viewing the scene for a moment in triumph, Trepov signals the policemen out and moves triumphantly after them. The Major stands looking up at the bodies and sadly shakes his head; then he, too, exits. On the other side of the stage, Vladimir also stares at the swinging bodies. Vera puts a comforting arm around his shoulder, but he thrusts it off and moves downstage.*)

VERA

(*concerned*) Vladimir . . (*He stands shaking with fury, and she moves to him. They are now alone onstage. The lights dim all around them, leaving them lighted and the silhouettes of the gently swaying bodies against the blue cyclorama above them.*)

VLADIMIR

I will revenge myself on them. Alexi wasn't like the others. He didn't kill anyone.

VERA

He was a revolutionary. These days, that's crime enough.

VLADIMIR

(*bitterly*) But what have *I* done? I'm no revolutionary, but they've expelled me from the University.

VERA

You're a liberal and your name is Ulyanov.

VLADIMIR

Then I'll change! (*pacing back and forth*) What a fool I was. I thought better laws could change things. What we need is civil war! (*The lights now fade slowly from the cyclorama, and the bodies disappear into the darkness.*)

VERA

Someday. But now, the cause is going underground. To plan and prepare.

VLADIMIR

Let me join you. Show me what to do.

VERA

(*studying him*) Yes, I could teach you the lessons Nechaev taught me.

VLADIMIR

I'll be a good disciple.

VERA

Do you understand what that means? (*He nods.*) And you're still willing to undertake Nechaev's cause? (*Cyclorama: slide or film montage — The*

209

Revolution Triumphs. As Vladimir says the following, we see shots of the Russian Bolshevik Revolution: crowds, speakers haranguing them, marches, red flags, troops, Cossack police, dead bodies, the battles of 1917, a family shot of the Romanoffs, the gruesome room where they were murdered. The last slide — timed to the speech — is one of Lenin, preferably a large, formal bust shot.)

VLADIMIR

(*with growing intensity*) Alexander Ulyanov is dead. From this day forward, so is his brother. In their place lives a new man with a new name — and nothing else. No family, no friends, no self. No pride or scruples or love. A man with the mercy torn out of him — dedicated to one end. Prepare yourself, Romanoffs! I am coming for you! The name of your executioner is Lenin! (*The light blinks out on him and Vera. Nechaev's flute plays. Cyclorama: Lenin's slide dissolves into the now gigantic slide of Nechaev, grinning at the audience. After a moment, Nechaev himself appears downstage in his spotlight to confront the audience. He carries the flute and smiles as in the picture. He is unchained and unmarked, appearing much the same as he did in the beginning. Cyclorama: the slide of Nechaev dims somewhat.*)

NECHAEV

That is my story — thus far. This is how the world of today was begun. The story is true. You saw it as it actually happened. The play does not end here, however. You go back to it as you leave here tonight. You go back to the world that I and Vera and Drovnik and Lenin have made for you. You go back to confront our disciples of today, who are creating the world for your children.

You cannot scoff at beards and wild rhetoric now . . nor slogans and demonstrations. You've seen what a ragged rabble, a mere handful of the dedicated can do. Overthrow a Czar? Take control of the largest landmass on the face of the globe? Exert our force on half of civilization? We shall do more! We shall control the entire world! (*Cyclorama: slide or film montage — rioting, destruction, death. Militant students, blacks, overturned cars and school buses, the King and Kennedy assassinations, shacks, slums, Biafran children, Vietnam. Through it all — or alongside — the slide of Nechaev can still dimly be seen.*)

You doubt it? Doubt no more. You are my greatest ally. Wherever there is hunger, wherever there is war or oppression, tyranny or injustice — there am I, reaping the fruits of your planting.

I feed on that dark side of you, I gorge myself on the evil in your hearts and minds. Every act of hate and wickedness strengthens me. Your weakness is my very power!

THE NIHILIST

"This is a play," you plead with yourself. "It can't really happen. It can't!"
It will! (*shouting*) I am the rising crest of the future. I am the tidal wave
of Tomorrow. I will sweep over you and destroy you! (*Cyclorama: the
montage has ended, and the Nechaev slide now dominates the stage again.
Nechaev pauses for effect, then laughs, and speaks gently.*) And there is
not one thing you can do about it! (*He laughs again, louder and louder,
standing in triumph before the audience. Cyclorama: as the match flares,
the slide blinks out. Suddenly, near him, or behind and above him on the
ramparts, a match flares in the darkness, illuminating the Major. He lights
his pipe and puffs until he is ringed in smoke. Sensing him, Nechaev stops
laughing and turns to face him tensely.*)

MAJOR

Perhaps . . (*The two antagonists look at each other for a long, hard moment;
then the Major smiles and blows out his match — and all light on the stage
blinks out.*)

THE END

The *Nihilist* by William N. Monson was presented March
10–14, 1971, at the Main Theatre, University of California,
Davis. It was directed by Alfred Rossi.

Cast of Characters

SERGEI NECHAEV	Jon Estrin
VERA ZASNER	Pat Estrin
PETER TKACHEV	Wayne Harrison
ANDREI DROVNIK	Paul Ford
SOFIA PEROVNA	Judith Schwartz
IVAN PRIZHOV	Brad Coleman
DMITRI KUZNETSOV	Joseph Fera
IVAN IVANOVICH IVANOV	Randy Pellish
ALEXANDER HERTZEN	Lance Jencks
NATALIE HERTZEN	Sarah DuPrau
MIKHAIL BAKUNIN	Robert Cello
NICHOLAS OGAREV	Michael Beevers
ALEXANDER ULYANOV	Mike Hanna
VLADIMIR	Martin Brifman
DUKE URUSOV	David Wright

THE CORPORAL	Kent Vanderbundt
THE MAJOR	Glenn Jackson
GENERAL TREPOV	Frank Pendle
THE CHANCELLOR	Jay Morse
THE JUDGE	Jay Morse
THE PROSECUTOR	Alan Stambusky
GRIGOR SHIRAEV	John Aden
STEPHEN KHALTURIN	Doug Street
SEMYON	Steve Majesky
THE LANDLADY	Ceva Bauer
THE GOVERNOR	Richard Bright

OTHER STUDENTS   Cynthia Darnell, Peggy Ferguson,
Dennis Breen, Marsha Vanderford, Janice Bishop,
Mary McKercher, Mark Wallner, Nancy Santa Maria,
Kenneth Komoto, Ralph deLaubenfels,
Doug Bassler, John Erickson

POLICEMEN   Bruce Bechtold, Steve Fross, Rick Mallett,
Jerome Callens, Pete Sarbeff, Josh Stein

(Note. In a revision of the play after the University of California, Davis, production, the parts of Shiraev, Khalturin, Semyon, the Landlady, and the Governor were eliminated or combined into the new character Kibalchich, which appears in the version published here.)